PRAISE FOR LUKE MARSH

The Daily History Trivia Challenge is a year-long mental workout that makes history feel like a grand, data-filled adventure.

— DR. LENA MORETTI, HISTORIAN AND EDUCATOR

366 daily challenges turn dates into stories you actually want to chase, and the deep dives are pure fascination.

— SAMIR CHEN, QUIZ SHOW PRODUCER

If you think you know history, this book will prove you wrong—every page expands your curiosity and sharpens your memory.

— RENEE CARTER, EDITOR AND BOOK REVIEWER

THE DAILY HISTORY TRIVIA CHALLENGE

THE DAILY HISTORY TRIVIA CHALLENGE

TEST YOUR KNOWLEDGE WITH 366 QUESTIONS, ANSWERS, AND FASCINATING BACKSTORIES FROM THIS DAY IN HISTORY

THE DAILY TRIVIA COLLECTION
BOOK ONE

LUKE MARSH

Want 100+ More Mind-Blowing Stories for Free?

Before you dive into the rest of this book, I have a quick gift for you.

As a thank you for reading, I've put together an exclusive collection of **100+ Interesting Real Stories** that you won't find anywhere else. It is the perfect bite-sized companion to keep the fascination going.

Here is how to get your free copy right now:
1. Open your smartphone camera.
2. Scan the QR code below.
3. Tell me where to send your free book!

Don't have a scanner handy? No problem. You can also download your gift directly at:

bookboundstudios.com/free/facts

Luke Marsh & The Team at Book Bound Studios

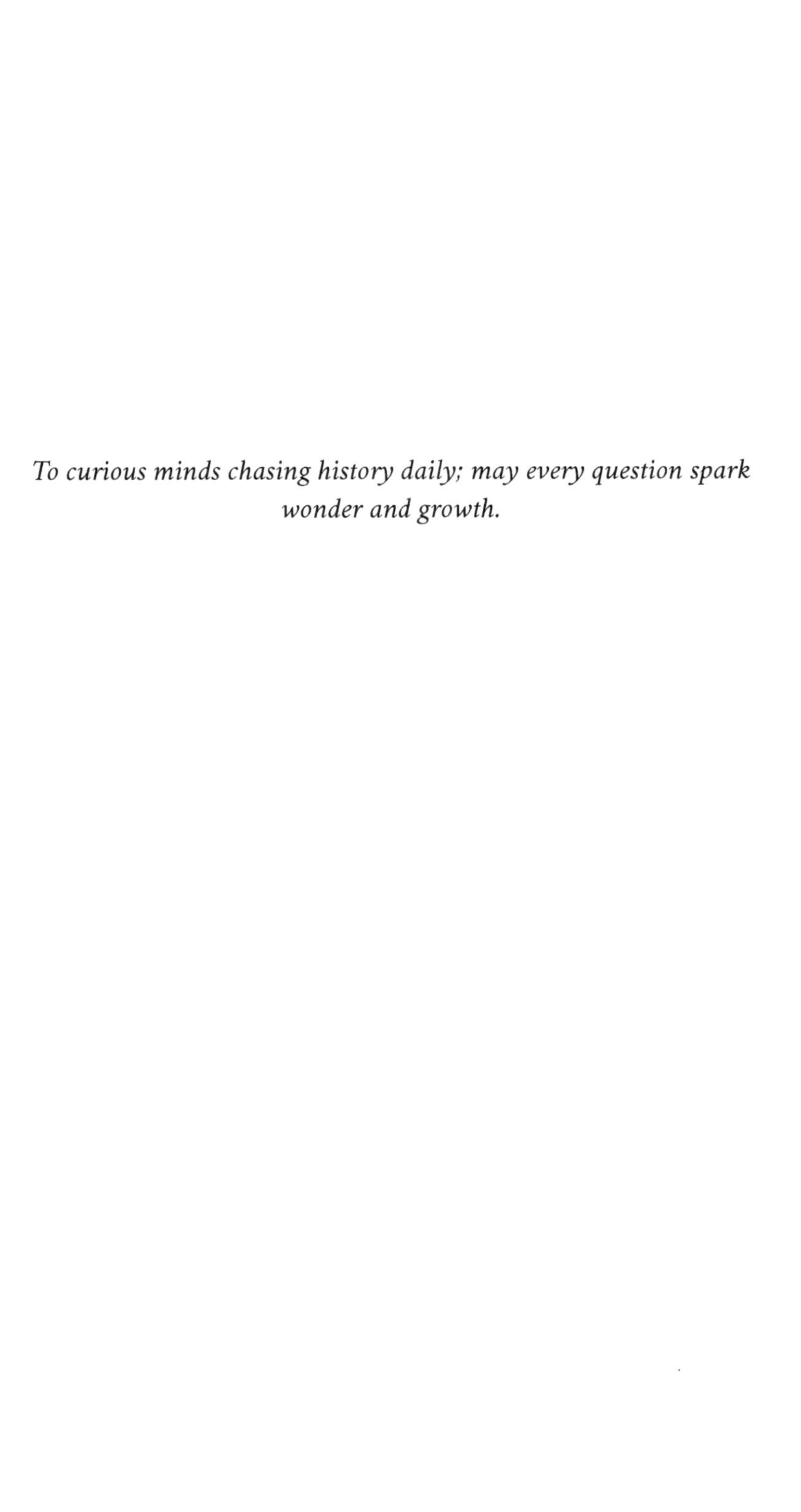

To curious minds chasing history daily; may every question spark wonder and growth.

Those who cannot remember the past are condemned
to repeat it.

— GEORGE SANTAYANA, THE LIFE OF REASON,

REASON IN COMMON SENSE (1905)

CONTENTS

INTRODUCTION

Welcome to The Daily History Trivia Challenge, your year-long mental workout. This isn't another dry chronicle—it's a gamified journey through time that makes history feel alive in bite-sized chunks.

Each day serves up a single, focused question about a historic event tied to that date. Try to answer before you peek at the answer, then read the succinct explanation to see how the story fits.

There are 366 daily challenges—yes, even for Leap Years—covering a wide range of topics and eras. Questions are intentionally varied, moving from empires and battles to culture, ideas, and quirky moments that illuminate the past.

This book is built for daily engagement: 5 to 15 minutes a day, a streak you can chase, and a habit that quietly expands your knowledge over time. It rewards consistency with crisp insights, quick dives, and those satisfying 'aha' moments.

Dive in and make history your daily ritual. Whether you're commuting, studying, or sharing trivia with friends, The Daily History Trivia Challenge is designed to spark curiosity and conversation—one question, one answer, one richer view of the world.

JANUARY

January 1

Question: On this day in 1804, which Caribbean colony declared independence after a successful slave revolt, becoming the first modern Black republic?

Answer: Haiti

On January 1st, 1804, Haiti declared independence from France, capping the only successful large-scale slave revolt in the Atlantic world. Leaders such as Jean-Jacques Dessalines helped turn a brutal plantation colony into a sovereign nation. The victory shattered assumptions about slavery's permanence and terrified slaveholding societies across the Americas. France later forced Haiti to pay a massive indemnity, a debt that crippled the new country's economy for generations. Haiti's revolution remains a landmark in human rights and anti-colonial history.

* * *

JANUARY 2

Question: On this day in 1492, which city did the Catholic Monarchs capture, completing the Reconquista in Spain?

Answer: Granada

On January 2nd, 1492, Granada surrendered to Ferdinand II of Aragon and Isabella I of Castile, ending centuries of Muslim rule in Iberia. The last Nasrid ruler, Muhammad XII (Boabdil), handed over the keys, closing the chapter of Al-Andalus as a political power. This victory unified much of Spain under Christian monarchs and reshaped its religious and cultural landscape. In the same year, the monarchy backed Columbus's voyage, helping launch Spain's global empire. Granada's fall is still a defining turning point in Spanish—and world—history.

* * *

JANUARY 3

Question: On this day in 1521, which religious reformer was formally excommunicated by Pope Leo X after refusing to recant his teachings?

Answer: Martin Luther

On January 3rd, 1521, Pope Leo X issued a bull excommunicating Martin Luther, severing him from the Catholic Church. Luther's critiques—especially of indulgences and papal authority—had already ignited fierce debate across Europe. The excommunication escalated the conflict and set the stage for the Diet of Worms later that year, where Luther famously refused to recant. His defiance accelerated the Protestant Reformation and fractured Western Christianity. The ripple effects reshaped politics, education, and religious life for centuries.

* * *

JANUARY 4

Question: On this day in 1959, which spacecraft became the first to reach the Moon, marking a major Soviet milestone in the Space Race?

Answer: Luna 1

On January 4th, 1959, the Soviet probe Luna 1 became the first spacecraft to reach the vicinity of the Moon. It missed a direct impact but flew past and entered a heliocentric orbit, proving the USSR could navigate beyond Earth. The mission delivered a powerful propaganda win during the Space Race, coming shortly after Sputnik's shock to the world. It also gathered early data on space radiation and the solar wind environment. Luna 1 helped turn lunar exploration from science fiction into a strategic reality.

* * *

JANUARY 5

Question: On this day in 1933, which massive engineering project began construction in San Francisco Bay, later becoming an icon of American design?

Answer: The Golden Gate Bridge

On January 5th, 1933, construction began on the Golden Gate Bridge, a daring project spanning the treacherous strait connecting San Francisco Bay to the Pacific. Engineer Joseph Strauss led the effort, while innovations in suspension design and safety measures helped make the job less deadly than many projects of its era. When it opened in 1937, the bridge dramatically improved transportation and commerce for the Bay Area. Its Art Deco styling and "International Orange" paint turned infrastructure into instant visual legend. Today it stands as a symbol of Depression-era ambition and engineering confidence.

JANUARY 6

Question: On this day in 1838, what communication technology made its first successful public demonstration when a message was sent along wires in a New Jersey lecture hall?

Answer: The telegraph

On January 6, 1838, Samuel Morse demonstrated a working electric telegraph at the Speedwell Ironworks in Morristown, New Jersey. His system used electrical pulses to move an electromagnet, laying the groundwork for Morse code and long-distance signaling. The telegraph dramatically shrank the time it took to share news, prices, and military information—from days to minutes. It became the nervous system of the 19th-century world, transforming commerce, journalism, and warfare.

* * *

JANUARY 7

Question: On this day in 1785, which English newspaper—still published today—was founded in London as the Daily Universal Register?

Answer: The Times

On January 7, 1785, the newspaper that would become The Times was founded in London under the name Daily Universal Register. Within a few years it rebranded as The Times, aiming for a sharper, more memorable identity. It grew into one of Britain's most influential papers, known for political coverage and foreign reporting. Its rise helped define the modern idea of a "paper of record" and shaped how the public consumed national and international news.

* * *

JANUARY 8

Question: On this day in 1815, which U.S. president's troops won the Battle of New Orleans, a major victory in the War of 1812 led by Andrew Jackson?

Answer: James Madison

On January 8, 1815, U.S. forces under Andrew Jackson won the Battle of New Orleans during the War of 1812—while President James Madison was still in office. The victory came after the Treaty of Ghent had been signed, but before news crossed the Atlantic, so the battle was fought as if the war were still raging. It boosted American morale, weakened

British leverage in the aftermath, and turned Jackson into a national hero. That fame became a political springboard, helping propel him to the presidency years later.

* * *

JANUARY 9

Question: On this day in 2007, which tech leader unveiled the first iPhone, pitching it as an iPod, a phone, and an internet communicator in one device?

Answer: Steve Jobs

On January 9, 2007, Steve Jobs introduced the first iPhone at the Macworld keynote in San Francisco. He framed it as three revolutionary products in one: a widescreen iPod, a mobile phone, and an internet communicator. The device's touch-first interface and app ecosystem soon reshaped how people work, shop, navigate, and socialize. It kicked off the modern smartphone era and forced nearly every major tech company to rethink its future.

* * *

JANUARY 10

Question: On this day in 49 BCE, which Roman leader crossed the Rubicon River, defying the Senate and triggering a civil war that would end the Roman Republic?

Answer: Julius Caesar

On January 10, 49 BCE, Julius Caesar crossed the Rubicon River with his legion, a direct challenge to the authority of the Roman Senate. Roman law effectively forbade a general from bringing an army into Italy, so the act was an unmistakable declaration of conflict. The decision ignited a civil war that ultimately left Caesar as dictator and shattered the Republic's political balance. "Crossing the Rubicon" still means passing a point of no return—because Caesar truly did.

* * *

JANUARY 11

Question: On this day in 1922, which life-saving medicine was first administered to a 14-year-old diabetic patient in Toronto, marking a turning point in the treatment of diabetes?

Answer: Insulin

On January 11, 1922, insulin was first given to 14-year-old Leonard Thompson at Toronto General Hospital, transforming a once-fatal diagnosis into a manageable condition. The early extract was refined quickly after initial issues, and the patient improved dramatically as purification methods advanced. The breakthrough is closely tied to Frederick Banting and Charles Best's lab work, with key support from J.J.R. Macleod and chemist James Collip. Within a few years, insulin production scaled up worldwide, saving millions of lives and reshaping modern endocrinology.

* * *

JANUARY 12

Question: On this day in 1967, which Jewish religious and cultural symbol premiered on television as the title character of a popular sitcom, becoming a landmark of representation in American pop culture?

Answer: A menorah (in "The Goldbergs")

On January 12, 1967, the sitcom "The Goldbergs" returned to television in a prime-time revival, and its cultural visibility helped bring Jewish family life into mainstream American living rooms. While the show had earlier radio and TV runs, its continued presence became a touchstone for everyday representation rather than exoticized stereotypes. By centering a warm, comedic household, it normalized traditions and immigrant experiences for broad audiences. Its legacy is often cited in discussions of how television shapes belonging—and who gets to be seen as "typical."

* * *

JANUARY 13

Question: On this day in 1898, which influential French writer published an open letter titled "J'Accuse…!" accusing the government of antisemitism and a miscarriage of justice in a major political scandal?

Answer: Émile Zola

On January 13, 1898, Émile Zola published "J'Accuse…!" in the newspaper L'Aurore, directly challenging France's leaders over the Dreyfus Affair. The letter accused the military and government of framing Captain Alfred Dreyfus and fueling antisemitic hysteria. Zola was prosecuted for libel and fled France, but the public pressure his writing generated helped keep the case alive. The affair ultimately exposed deep fractures in French society and became a defining moment for civil rights, journalism, and modern political activism.

January 14

Question: On this day in 1784, which governing body formally ratified the Treaty of Paris, officially ending the American Revolutionary War?

Answer: The U.S. Congress (Confederation Congress)

On January 14, 1784, the Confederation Congress ratified the Treaty of Paris, confirming the new United States as an independent nation. The treaty recognized U.S. sovereignty and set boundaries that stretched to the Mississippi River—an enormous territorial gain. Ratification also signaled the young country's entry into formal international diplomacy, even as it struggled under the weak Articles of Confederation. The peace it secured opened the door to westward expansion and intensified debates over how the nation should govern itself.

* * *

JANUARY 15

Question: On this day in 1559, which English monarch was crowned at Westminster Abbey, beginning a reign that reshaped religion, politics, and global power?

Answer: Elizabeth I

On January 15, 1559, Elizabeth I was crowned Queen of England at Westminster Abbey, launching one of the most iconic reigns in European history. Early in her rule, she steered the country toward a Protestant settlement designed to stabilize a nation whiplashed by religious conflict. Her era saw major cultural flourishing—think Shakespeare and the Elizabethan theater—and rising naval ambition. By the time her reign ended, England had strengthened its national identity and positioned itself for expansion on the world stage.

* * *

JANUARY 16

Question: On this day in 1920, what constitutional amendment took effect in the United States, banning the manufacture and sale of alcoholic beverages nationwide?

Answer: The 18th Amendment

On January 16, 1920, the 18th Amendment took effect, launching the era of Prohibition in the United States. Backed by decades of temperance activism, it aimed to curb crime, poverty, and domestic abuse by drying out the country. Instead, demand didn't disappear—it went underground, fueling speakeasies, bootlegging networks, and the rise of organized crime. Enforcement proved costly and uneven, and public support steadily eroded. The experiment ended in 1933 with the 21st Amendment, the only amendment to repeal another.

* * *

JANUARY 17

Question: On this day in 1991, which U.S.-led military operation began with a massive air campaign to drive Iraqi forces out of Kuwait?

Answer: Operation Desert Storm

On January 17, 1991, Operation Desert Storm began with a sweeping air assault against Iraq, marking the combat phase of the Gulf War. The campaign followed Iraq's 1990 invasion and annexation of Kuwait, which triggered a broad international coalition response. Precision-guided munitions and round-the-clock strikes showcased a new style of high-tech warfare to the world's TV screens. After weeks of bombing, a brief ground offensive routed Iraqi forces and liberated Kuwait. The conflict reshaped U.S. military doctrine and left lasting geopolitical tensions in the region.

* * *

JANUARY 18

Question: On this day in 1778, which English navigator became the first European recorded to sight the Hawaiian Islands, naming them the "Sandwich Islands"?

Answer: Captain James Cook

On January 18, 1778, Captain James Cook sighted the Hawaiian Islands, introducing the archipelago to European maps and empires. He called them the "Sandwich Islands" after the Earl of Sandwich, his patron back in Britain. Cook's arrival opened a new era of trade, missionaries, and imperial competition in the Pacific—along with devastating epidemics that Indigenous Hawaiians had no immunity against. His return to Hawai'i the following year ended in violence at Kealakekua Bay, where Cook was killed. The encounter became a pivot point in Hawaiian history and the broader story of Pacific colonization.

* * *

January 19

Question: On this day in 1809, which writer was born in Boston and later published "The Raven" and "The Tell-Tale Heart"?

Answer: Edgar Allan Poe

On January 19, 1809, Edgar Allan Poe was born in Boston, a future master of American gothic and psychological horror. His tales of obsession, guilt, and unraveling minds helped define modern short fiction and inspired generations of writers. Poe was also a sharp literary critic and an early pioneer of detective storytelling, laying groundwork for the genre later popularized by Sherlock Holmes. Despite his influence, he struggled financially and faced personal tragedies throughout his life. Today, his work remains a fixture of classrooms, pop culture, and any good late-night creep-out read.

* * *

JANUARY 20

Question: On this day in 1942, which group of senior Nazi officials met near Berlin to coordinate the logistics of the "Final Solution" in a conference later named for its location?

Answer: The Wannsee Conference

On January 20, 1942, the Wannsee Conference took place in a villa outside Berlin, where senior Nazi officials coordinated the administrative machinery of genocide. The meeting, chaired by Reinhard Heydrich, focused on deporting Europe's Jews and organizing mass murder across occupied territories. Its chilling minutes reveal how bureaucratic language was used to mask atrocities with terms like "evacuation" and "special treatment." While the Holocaust was already underway, Wannsee accelerated coordination across ministries and police agencies. The conference has become a stark symbol of how modern paperwork and planning can be weaponized for inhuman ends.

* * *

JANUARY 21

Question: On this day in 1924, which recently deceased Russian leader's body was placed on public display in a mausoleum in Moscow's Red Square?

Answer: Vladimir Lenin

On January 21, 1924, Vladimir Lenin died after a series of strokes, ending the life of the man who led the Bolshevik Revolution and helped create the Soviet state. Soviet leaders quickly turned his death into a political symbol, preserving his body and placing it in a mausoleum on Red Square. The public display helped cement a near-religious cult of personality around Lenin and the revolution. His passing also intensified the power struggle that ultimately brought Joseph Stalin to the top. The mausoleum remains one of the most iconic—and controversial—monuments of the 20th century.

* * *

JANUARY 22

Question: On this day in 1963, which Franco-German treaty was signed to promote reconciliation and cooperation after centuries of rivalry and two world wars?

Answer: Élysée Treaty

On January 22, 1963, France and West Germany signed the Élysée Treaty, a landmark agreement championed by Charles de Gaulle and Konrad Adenauer. It created regular consultations on foreign policy, defense, and education, aiming to lock in cooperation rather than conflict. The treaty helped transform two historic enemies into the engine room of European integration. It also boosted youth exchanges and cultural ties, making reconciliation tangible for ordinary citizens. Many historians see it as a cornerstone for today's European Union's Franco-German partnership.

* * *

JANUARY 23

Question: On this day in 1556, which Chinese emperor died, leaving behind a reign associated with the most lethal earthquake in recorded history?

Answer: Jiajing Emperor

On January 23, 1556, the Jiajing Emperor of the Ming dynasty died after a long and turbulent reign. That same date is forever linked to the Shaanxi earthquake, widely considered the deadliest recorded, with catastrophic losses across northern China. While the quake wasn't caused by the emperor, the coincidence of timing and the era's crises helped imprint the day in historical memory. Jiajing's rule was marked by court intrigue, costly policies, and mounting stresses on the dynasty. The disaster underscored how vulnerable even powerful empires were to nature's sudden violence.

* * *

JANUARY 24

Question: On this day in 1848, what precious-metal discovery at Sutter's Mill triggered a massive migration and economic boom in the American West?

Answer: Gold

On January 24, 1848, gold was discovered at Sutter's Mill near Coloma, California, by James W. Marshall. News spread slowly at first, then exploded into the California Gold Rush, drawing "Forty-Niners" from across the United States and the world. The sudden population surge accelerated California's path to statehood and transformed San Francisco into a booming hub. It also brought brutal consequences, especially for Indigenous communities who faced displacement, violence, and disease. The rush reshaped the American economy and helped cement the idea of the West as a land of risky opportunity.

* * *

January 25

Question: On this day in 1533, which English king secretly married Anne Boleyn, setting the stage for England's break with Rome?

Answer: Henry VIII

On January 25, 1533, Henry VIII married Anne Boleyn in secret, a turning point in English—and European—religious history. The marriage was politically explosive because Henry's first marriage to Catherine of Aragon had not been annulled by the pope. To secure his new union and a male heir, Henry pushed England toward a break with papal authority, leading to the English Reformation. Anne's rise also intensified court factionalism and religious change, even as her position remained precarious. Within three years she would be executed, but the institutional rupture she helped catalyze endured for centuries.

JANUARY 26

Question: On this day in 1788, what British colony became the first European settlement in Australia when the First Fleet raised the Union flag at Sydney Cove?

Answer: New South Wales

On January 26, 1788, Captain Arthur Phillip proclaimed the colony of New South Wales at Sydney Cove, marking the start of permanent British settlement in Australia. The First Fleet had arrived with convicts, soldiers, and supplies to establish a penal colony far from Britain. For many Australians today, the date is observed as Australia Day— while also being a day of mourning for many Indigenous peoples, who call it "Invasion Day." The anniversary continues to shape national debates about identity, colonization, and reconciliation.

* * *

JANUARY 27

Question: On this day in 1945, which Soviet military camp was liberated, revealing the world's most notorious system of Nazi mass murder?

Answer: Auschwitz

On January 27, 1945, Soviet troops liberated Auschwitz, the largest Nazi concentration and extermination camp complex. They found surviving prisoners, vast stores of victims' belongings, and evidence of industrial-scale murder. The liberation became a defining moment in the world's understanding of the Holocaust's magnitude. Today, the date is commemorated internationally as Holocaust Remembrance Day, a stark reminder of where hatred and state power can lead.

* * *

JANUARY 28

Question: On this day in 1986, which space shuttle broke apart shortly after liftoff, killing all seven crew members and shocking live TV audiences?

Answer: Challenger

On January 28, 1986, the Space Shuttle Challenger disintegrated 73 seconds after launch, killing all seven astronauts aboard. The disaster was traced largely to failure of O-rings in a solid rocket booster, made worse by unusually cold temperatures. It forced NASA to pause shuttle flights and overhaul safety culture, design, and decision-making processes. The tragedy also reshaped how the public viewed spaceflight—still inspiring awe, but with a clearer sense of its risks.

* * *

JANUARY 29

Question: On this day in 1845, what U.S. newspaper title—still published today—was founded in New York City with the motto "All the News That's Fit to Print"?

Answer: The New York Times

On January 29, 1851, The New York Times (originally the New-York Daily Times) published its first issue in New York City. It aimed to distinguish itself from sensational "penny press" papers with a reputation for more sober reporting. Over time, it became one of the world's most influential newspapers, shaping political discourse and investigative journalism. Its reporting and editorial voice have played major roles in everything from wartime coverage to modern media accountability.

JANUARY 30

Question: On this day in 1933, which German political figure was appointed chancellor—an appointment that rapidly dismantled democracy and set Europe on a path to war?

Answer: Adolf Hitler

On January 30, 1933, Adolf Hitler was appointed chancellor of Germany by President Paul von Hindenburg. Conservative elites believed they could control him, but the appointment gave the Nazis a platform to seize power legally and then crush opposition. Within months, civil liberties were suspended and Germany moved toward a one-party dictatorship. The consequences were catastrophic: the Holocaust, World War II, and a reshaped global order in the war's aftermath.

JANUARY 31

Question: On this day in 1865, which amendment to the U.S. Constitution passed Congress, formally setting the nation on a path to abolish slavery?

Answer: The 13th Amendment

On January 31, 1865, the U.S. House of Representatives approved the 13th Amendment, clearing the final major hurdle in Congress to abolish slavery nationwide. The Senate had already passed it, but the House vote was tense—won only after intense lobbying and shifting political alliances in the final months of the Civil War. The amendment then went to the states for ratification, becoming law later that year. Its passage marked a constitutional turning point, ending legal slavery in the United States and redefining the meaning of freedom after the war. Even so, it also set the stage for new battles over civil rights and equality during Reconstruction and beyond.

2

FEBRUARY

February 1

Question: Which protest action began on this day in 1960 when four students sat at a segregated lunch counter in Greensboro, North Carolina?

Answer: Greensboro sit-ins

On February 1st, 1960, four students from North Carolina A&T State University sat at a Woolworth's lunch counter in Greensboro, challenging the store's Jim Crow policies. Their quiet, nonviolent act drew attention and inspired others to join, sparking a wave of sit-ins across the South. The protests pressured businesses to desegregate and energized the broader Civil Rights Movement. This moment demonstrated how small, organized actions could catalyze national change. It helped lay the groundwork for landmark civil rights legislation in the 1960s.

* * *

FEBRUARY 2

Question: What treaty ended the Mexican-American War on this day in 1848?

Answer: Treaty of Guadalupe Hidalgo

On February 2nd, 1848, the Treaty of Guadalupe Hidalgo was signed, ending the Mexican-American War. Mexico ceded vast swaths of territory to the United States, including present-day California, Nevada, Utah, and parts of several other states. In return, the United States paid Mexico $15 million and honored claims of American citizens against Mexico. The treaty dramatically reshaped the map of North America and spurred a new era of westward expansion. It also intensified debates over the spread of slavery into new territories.

* * *

FEBRUARY 3

Question: What event on this day in 1959 became known as the Day the Music Died?

Answer: Buddy Holly plane crash

On February 3rd, 1959, a small plane carrying Buddy Holly, Ritchie Valens, and the Big Bopper crashed near Clear Lake, Iowa. The tragedy ended the lives of three up-and-coming rock 'n' roll stars and stunned fans around the world. Radio and record charts mourned the loss, and the incident became a cultural touchstone for the era. The phrase 'the day the music died' captured the sense of abrupt, youthful loss. Holly's influence, however, lived on through his recordings and the later generations of artists he inspired.

* * *

FEBRUARY 4

Question: What social network launched on this day in 2004, initially at Harvard?

Answer: Facebook

On February 4th, 2004, Facebook launched from Harvard University as TheFacebook. It quickly expanded to other colleges and then opened to the general public, transforming how people connect online. Its early focus on real-name profiles and college networks helped shape online social behavior and data privacy discussions for years to come. The platform evolved into a global communications and media ecosystem, impacting journalism, politics, marketing, and everyday social life. Its rapid growth spurred a new wave of social media platforms and a revolution in digital culture.

* * *

FEBRUARY 5

Question: Which document was adopted on this day in 1849 to lay the groundwork for California's state government?

Answer: California Constitution

On February 5th, 1849, California adopted its first constitution during a constitutional convention in Monterey. This foundational document established the framework for California's state government, laws, and governance as the territory prepared for statehood. Voters would eventually ratify it, paving the way for California's admission to the Union in 1850. The constitution reflected the ambitions and tensions of a rapidly growing frontier society and set the stage for California's political development. It remains a pivotal moment in the state's path from territory to statehood.

February 6

Question: On this day in 1952, who became monarch of the United Kingdom after the death of George VI?

Answer: Elizabeth II

On February 6, 1952, Elizabeth II ascended to the throne after the death of her father, King George VI. Her coronation would take place on June 2, 1953. Her accession marked a new era for the British monarchy as it navigated postwar changes. As monarch, she presided over decades of change, from decolonization to the modern Commonwealth. Elizabeth's long reign became a defining symbol of continuity for Britain and the Commonwealth in a rapidly changing world.

February 7

Question: On this day in 1964, which legendary band landed in the United States, sparking Beatlemania?

Answer: The Beatles

On February 7, 1964, the Beatles touched down at New York's Kennedy Airport, beginning their first U.S. tour. The arrival followed months of growing fame in Britain and Europe. Two days later, they performed on The Ed Sullivan Show, delivering a performance that electrified the U.S. The performances helped catalyze Beatlemania and a seismic shift in global pop culture. They cemented their place in music history and cultural history.

* * *

FEBRUARY 8

Question: On this day in 1910, which youth organization was founded in the United States?

Answer: Boy Scouts of America

On February 8, 1910, the Boy Scouts of America was founded by William D. Boyce and others. The movement quickly spread with a framework of outdoor skills, citizenship, and service. It mirrored evolving ideas about childhood, independence, and civic duty in early 20th-century America. The organization would expand into a global network and diversify, while preserving its core ethos of 'be prepared'. The Boy Scouts of America would leave a lasting imprint on youth development and community service.

* * *

FEBRUARY 9

Question: On this day in 1825, which man was selected as President by the House of Representatives after the disputed 1824 election?

Answer: John Quincy Adams

On February 9, 1825, the House awarded the presidency to John Quincy Adams after Andrew Jackson won a plurality but not majority in the Electoral College. Critics labeled the outcome the 'Corrupt Bargain,' shaping early American party politics. Adams's presidency faced intense opposition from Jackson and his supporters, influencing policy and elections for years. Adams advocated modernization and infrastructure improvements, including the American System, though he had limited political capital. The 1825 decision set a precedent for how close elections could be resolved when no candidate had a majority.

$$* * *$$

FEBRUARY 10

Question: On this day in 1763, which treaty ended the Seven Years' War?

Answer: Treaty of Paris

On February 10, 1763, the Treaty of Paris ended the global conflict known as the Seven Years' War. By its terms, France ceded Canada and most of its territories in North America to Britain, reshaping colonial power. The settlement also adjusted territories in India and the Caribbean in favor of Britain and its allies. The war's end reshaped geopolitics and sowed seeds of tensions that would echo into the American Revolution. The Treaty of Paris helped define the map of colonial empires for years to come.

* * *

FEBRUARY 11

Question: On this day in 1990, which anti-apartheid leader was released from prison?

Answer: Nelson Mandela

On February 11, 1990, Nelson Mandela walked out of Victor Verster Prison, signaling a turning point in South Africa's eight-decade struggle against apartheid. International pressure and internal reforms had converged to push the system toward reform. Mandela, who had spent 27 years in prison, became a central figure in the transition toward multiracial democracy. The moment reshaped South Africa's future and inspired anti-apartheid movements worldwide.

* * *

FEBRUARY 12

Question: On this day in 1809, which future U.S. president was born?

Answer: Abraham Lincoln

On February 12, 1809, Abraham Lincoln was born in a log cabin in Kentucky, a childhood marked by hardship and frontier life. He would grow into the leader who steered the United States through its Civil War. Lincoln's Emancipation

Proclamation and his pursuit to preserve the Union reshaped American history. His eloquence and leadership continue to shape debates about rights and democracy.

* * *

FEBRUARY 13

Question: On this day in 1633, which Italian astronomer faced the Inquisition for defending heliocentrism?

Answer: Galileo Galilei

On February 13, 1633, Galileo Galilei confronted the Roman Inquisition over his support for Copernican heliocentrism. The church forced him to recant his views under threat of torture; his abjuration became a symbol of the clash between science and religious authority. The proceedings cast a long shadow on scientific inquiry, but also prompted later generations to reexamine the evidence for heliocentrism. Galileo's legacy lived on in the slow, hard-won acceptance of astronomical truths that we accept today.

* * *

FEBRUARY 14

Question: On this day in 1876, which invention received the U.S. patent from Alexander Graham Bell?

Answer: Telephone

On February 14, 1876, Alexander Graham Bell was awarded the U.S. patent for the invention of the telephone. Bell's device turned voice into signals that could be transmitted over copper wires, shrinking distances. The patent sparked a race and a revolution in communication technology. The telephone catalyzed a century of innovations in telecommunication, reshaping business, government, and daily life.

* * *

FEBRUARY 15

Question: On this day in 1898, which U.S. warship exploded in Havana harbor, sparking the Spanish-American War?

Answer: USS Maine

On February 15, 1898, the battleship USS Maine exploded in Havana harbor, killing 260 sailors. The incident inflamed American public opinion against Spain and became a rallying cry for war. Investigations would blame internal magazine explosions rather than deliberate attack, but the event helped propel U.S. intervention in Cuba. The Spanish-American War reshaped the U.S. role on the world stage, signaling a new era of American power in the Caribbean and Pacific.

* * *

FEBRUARY 16

Question: Who was born in Hodgenville, Kentucky, who would become the 16th president of the United States?

Answer: Abraham Lincoln

On February 16, 1809, Abraham Lincoln was born in Hodgenville, Kentucky. He grew from frontier beginnings into a lawyer and leader who would become the 16th president. He steered the nation through the Civil War and issued the Emancipation Proclamation, redefining the war's purpose around ending slavery. Lincoln's legacy reshaped American democracy and the ongoing fight for equal rights.

* * *

FEBRUARY 17

Question: Which opera by Giacomo Puccini premiered in Milan and would become one of the most-performed works in the operatic repertoire?

Answer: Madama Butterfly

On February 17, 1904, Puccini's Madama Butterfly premiered in Milan. The production astonished audiences with its stark, tragic arc and cultural controversy. Although critics and audiences initially balked, the opera was revised and relaunched in 1907 to become a staple of the repertoire. Today, its melodies, heartbreak, and dramatic irony continue to captivate opera houses around the world.

* * *

FEBRUARY 18

Question: What celestial body was discovered on this day by Clyde Tombaugh?

Answer: Pluto

On February 18, 1930, Clyde Tombaugh at Lowell Observatory confirmed the existence of Pluto. This distant world added a ninth planet to the catalog of the solar system —the orbits beyond Neptune had scientists buzzing. For decades, Pluto was treated as a full planet, until 2006, when the IAU redefined the category and reclassified Pluto as a dwarf planet. The once-controversial classification sparked debates about what counts as a 'planet,' and kept Pluto in the public imagination as a frontier of discovery.

FEBRUARY 19

Question: What executive order, signed during World War II, authorized the internment of tens of thousands of Japanese Americans?

Answer: Executive Order 9066

On February 19, 1942, President Franklin D. Roosevelt signed Executive Order 9066. This order authorized the forced relocation and internment of tens of thousands of Japanese Americans during World War II. The policy shattered families and communities, exposing civil liberties to wartime fear. In later decades, the United States confronted the injustice with apologies and redress programs.

FEBRUARY 20

Question: Who became the first American to orbit the Earth during the Mercury-Atlas 6 mission?

Answer: John Glenn

On February 20, 1962, John Glenn became the first American to orbit the Earth aboard Friendship 7. The three-orbit flight showcased U.S. space prowess during the tense early years of the Space Race. The mission ended with a splashdown in the Atlantic and a hero's welcome for Glenn. His solo orbit inspired a generation of scientists, engineers, and dreamers to reach further.

* * *

FEBRUARY 21

Question: What influential political pamphlet did Karl Marx and Friedrich Engels publish on this day in 1848?

Answer: The Communist Manifesto

On February 21, 1848, The Communist Manifesto was published in London by the Communist League, co-authored by Karl Marx and Friedrich Engels. Its opening line —the history of all hitherto existing society is the history of class struggles—set a bold framework for understanding social change. The pamphlet argued for the overthrow of capitalist systems and the establishment of a classless society. Its influence rippled through worker movements across Europe and beyond, shaping socialist and communist ideologies for generations.

* * *

FEBRUARY 22

Question: Which future U.S. president was born on this day in 1732?

Answer: George Washington

On February 22, 1732, George Washington was born in Westmoreland County, Virginia. He would go on to serve as the commander-in-chief of the Continental Army during the American Revolutionary War. Washington helped steer the creation of a new American republic and set iconic precedents for the young nation. His leadership and vision left a lasting imprint on the U.S. Constitution and national identity.

* * *

FEBRUARY 23

Question: What iconic photograph was taken on this day in 1945 during the Battle of Iwo Jima?

Answer: Iwo Jima flag-raising

On February 23, 1945, U.S. Marines raised a flag atop Mount Suribachi on Iwo Jima, an image captured by photographer Joe Rosenthal that became one of the most enduring symbols of World War II. The photograph won the Pulitzer Prize and helped boost public morale during a brutal island campaign. The moment was quickly stitched into posters, stamps, and war bonds, shaping American memory of the war. The broader Iwo Jima operation provided the Marines with a crucial air and naval base against Japan, contributing to the war's outcome.

* * *

FEBRUARY 24

Question: Which U.S. president was impeached by the House on this day in 1868?

Answer: Andrew Johnson

On February 24, 1868, the U.S. House of Representatives voted to impeach President Andrew Johnson. The charges centered on his approach to Reconstruction and clashes with Congress over Civil rights and military rule in the former Confederacy. Johnson's Senate trial would end in acquittal by a single vote, leaving him in office. The impeachment highlighted the fraught power balance between the presidency and Congress during Reconstruction.

* * *

FEBRUARY 25

Question: Who became the first Black U.S. Senator taking office on this day in 1870?

Answer: Hiram Rhodes Revels

On February 25, 1870, Hiram Rhodes Revels was sworn in as the first Black United States Senator. He filled the Mississippi seat left vacant by Jefferson Davis. Revels's milestone marked a landmark moment in Reconstruction and civil rights history. His service opened doors for Black political representation, shaping the path of American democracy.

* * *

FEBRUARY 26

Question: On this day in 1815, which leader escaped from Elba and sparked the Hundred Days?

Answer: Napoleon Bonaparte

On February 26, 1815, Napoleon Bonaparte escaped from Elba and began his dramatic return to power. He landed in France with a small force and quickly regained support among soldiers and officials weary of the Bourbon Restoration. By March he had entered Paris and the Hundred Days were underway. The campaign culminated in the decisive defeat at Waterloo, ending Napoleon's bid for a renewed empire. The episode destabilized Europe, forcing the allied powers to redraw the map at the Congress of Vienna and shape politics for the rest of the century.

* * *

FEBRUARY 27

Question: On this day in 1933, which major fire in Berlin helped Adolf Hitler consolidate power?

Answer: Reichstag Fire

On February 27, 1933, the Reichstag building in Berlin was set ablaze. Hitler exploited the blaze to push the Reichstag Fire Decree, suspending civil liberties and allowing mass arrests of political opponents. The decree weakened the Weimar Constitution and paved the way for the Enabling Act, which gave Hitler's government emergency powers. Within weeks, the Nazi regime had eliminated rivals and solidified dictatorship across Germany.

* * *

February 28

Question: On this day in 1953, which two scientists announced they had discovered the double-helix structure of DNA?

Answer: James Watson and Francis Crick

On February 28, 1953, James Watson and Francis Crick announced that they had deduced the double-helix structure of DNA. Their model explained how genetic information could be replicated and stored, a cornerstone of modern biology. They relied on X-ray diffraction data from Rosalind Franklin and Maurice Wilkins, whose contributions were crucial. The discovery sparked a molecular biology revolution, enabling genetics, biotech, and advances in medicine.

* * *

February 29

Question: On this day in 1504, which navigator reputedly used a lunar eclipse to persuade indigenous people to continue supplying him?

Answer: Christopher Columbus

On February 29, 1504, Christopher Columbus, stranded in Jamaica, reputedly forecast a lunar eclipse to terrify the local population into providing him with food and shelter. The trick hinged on a fearsome omen and a show of astronomical knowledge. According to the tale, the locals relented and extended assistance until the crisis passed. The episode has become a famous anecdote about explorers, myth, and the fragile balance of power in early colonial encounters.

3

MARCH

March 1

Question: On this day in 1872, which national park was established as the first of its kind in the United States?

Answer: Yellowstone National Park

On March 1st, 1872, Yellowstone National Park was established by act of Congress, making it the first national park in the United States. Preservation goals accompanied the creation, prioritizing iconic geysers and wild landscapes over commercial development. Ranchers and miners soon learned that the park would require new kinds of management. The designation helped spark a global conservation movement. Today, Yellowstone's geothermal wonders and diverse ecosystems continue to draw millions of visitors and inspire researchers.

* * *

MARCH 2

Question: On this day in 1961, which organization was established to promote international volunteer service?

Answer: Peace Corps

On March 1st, 1961, the Peace Corps was established to promote world peace and friendship through volunteer service. President John F. Kennedy announced the initiative as a way to foster goodwill and practical humanitarian aid abroad. Volunteers were sent to teach, build, and assist communities in developing nations. The program grew into a symbol of American civic diplomacy during the Cold War era. Today, the Peace Corps has sent hundreds of thousands of volunteers and left a lasting cross-cultural exchange.

* * *

MARCH 3

Question: On this day in 1807, which act did Congress pass to ban the importation of enslaved people into the United States?

Answer: Act Prohibiting Importation of Slaves

On March 2, 1807, the Act Prohibiting Importation of Slaves was signed into law. That law ended formal importation of enslaved people, though slavery itself persisted in many states. It took effect in 1808 and reshaped the slave trade routes and enforcement practices. A generation of abolitionists used its passage to push further emancipation. The act stands as a landmark step in the long, painful road toward ending slavery in the United States.

* * *

MARCH 4

Question: On this day in 1789, which governing framework began operation, creating a new government in the United States?

Answer: U.S. Constitution

On March 4, 1789, the United States began operating under the Constitution as the first Congress convened in New York. Its framework established a system of checks and balances across three branches. The moment marked a transition from the Articles of Confederation to a stronger federal government. This event laid the bedrock for a durable constitutional republic. Today, the Constitution remains the supreme law of the land and a core symbol of American civic life.

* * *

MARCH 5

Question: On this day in 1953, which Soviet leader died, triggering leadership transitions in the USSR?

Answer: Joseph Stalin

On March 5, 1953, Joseph Stalin died at the age of 74 after decades of rule. His death opened a power vacuum that accelerated leadership changes within the Soviet hierarchy. Khrushchev and others would maneuver to push through reform and de-Stalinization in the coming years. Stalin's legacy shaped Soviet policy, paranoia, and the Cold War dynamic for years to come. His passing marked the end of an era and reshaped the future of postwar geopolitics.

* * *

MARCH 6

Question: On this day in 1957, which country became the first sub-Saharan colony to gain independence?

Answer: Ghana

On March 6, 1957, Ghana declared independence from British rule, marking a turning point in Africa's decolonization era. Led by Kwame Nkrumah, Ghana's move inspired other colonies across the continent to pursue self-rule. The new nation established a republic soon after and became a beacon for Pan-Africanism. Its independence helped catalyze a wave of decolonization that reshaped global politics in the second half of the 20th century. March 6, 1957, is remembered as a milestone in the rise of sovereign African nations.

* * *

MARCH 7

Question: Who spoke the first successful telephone call on this day in 1876?

Answer: Alexander Graham Bell

On March 7, 1876, Alexander Graham Bell spoke the words to his assistant, 'Mr. Watson, come here—I want you.' The moment proved that voice could travel over a wire. Bell's success led to the patent and a communications revolution. The invention rapidly spread, enabling business, journalism, and personal life to shrink distances. The patent marked the birth of modern telecommunications.

* * *

MARCH 8

Question: What city did the 1917 women's day protests begin in that helped trigger the Russian Revolution?

Answer: Petrograd

On March 8, 1917, protests began in Petrograd as workers demanded bread, peace, and an end to autocracy. The unrest quickly grew into a broader revolutionary movement that forced Tsar Nicholas II to abdicate. This sequence paved the way for a provisional government and the rise of Soviet power in the years that followed. The events reverberated across the world, fueling anti-imperial and labor movements for decades. Petrograd's streets became a symbol of mass political awakening.

* * *

MARCH 9

Question: What iconic fashion doll did Mattel introduce on this day in 1959?

Answer: Barbie

On March 9, 1959, Barbie debuted at the American International Toy Fair in New York. Created by Ruth

Handler, she embodied a shift toward modern, fashion-conscious play for girls. Barbie sparked conversations about beauty standards, careers, and gender roles that continue today. The doll quickly became a cultural phenomenon, spawning a vast ecosystem of toys, media, and merchandise. Barbie's launch reshaped the toy industry and popular culture.

* * *

MARCH 10

Question: What device did Alexander Graham Bell receive a patent for on this day in 1876?

Answer: Telephone

On March 10, 1876, Bell's patent for the telephone was granted, sealing a breakthrough in communication technology. The device translated vocal vibrations into electrical signals that could travel along wires to a distant receiver. This invention transformed business, journalism, and daily life by enabling near-instant conversations across space. It launched a century-long cascade of communications innovations—from landlines to mobile networks and the Internet. The patent marked the dawn of a truly connected world.

* * *

MARCH 11

Question: On this day in 2011, what natural disaster struck off the coast of Japan and triggered a devastating tsunami?

Answer: Tohoku earthquake

On March 11, 2011, a magnitude 9.0 earthquake struck off Japan's northeast coast, generating a monstrous tsunami. The waves devastated coastal communities and sparked the Fukushima Daiichi nuclear crisis. Emergency responders and international aid rushed to assist, though recovery would take years. The disaster prompted sweeping reforms in disaster preparedness, energy policy, and nuclear safety around the world.

* * *

MARCH 12

Question: On this day in 1933, what form of radio address did Franklin D. Roosevelt deliver for the first time to reassure the nation?

Answer: Fireside chat

On March 12, 1933, Roosevelt spoke to the American public in his first fireside chat, a direct radio address designed to feel like a conversation by the hearth. He explained banking reforms and the New Deal in plain language, aiming to calm the public during the Great Depression. The intimate, homey format helped restore public confidence and trust in government. The fireside chat became a lasting model for presidential communication and public diplomacy.

* * *

MARCH 13

Question: On this day in 1938, which country did Nazi Germany annex?

Answer: Austria

On March 13, 1938, Nazi Germany annexed Austria, an event known as the Anschluss. The takeover erased Austrian sovereignty and aligned Austria with the Third Reich. The annexation escalated European tensions and advanced Hitler's expansionist aims. It provoked international condemnation and contributed to the climate that led to World War II.

* * *

MARCH 14

Question: On this day in 1900, which act established gold as the standard for U.S. currency?

Answer: Gold Standard Act

On March 14, 1900, the Gold Standard Act formalized the shift to a gold-backed currency for the United States. It fixed the value of the dollar to a specific amount of gold and limited the role of silver in monetary policy. The act provided monetary stability for decades, shaping economic policy across administrations. It remained in effect until the United States moved away from the gold standard in the 1930s.

* * *

MARCH 15

Question: On this day in 44 BCE, which Roman leader was assassinated in the Senate?

Answer: Julius Caesar

On March 15, 44 BCE, Julius Caesar was assassinated by a group of senators. The murder intensified political rivalries and precipitated the end of the Roman Republic. Caesar's death triggered civil war and the rise of Emperor Augustus. The Ides of March became a lasting symbol of betrayal and political plotting.

* * *

MARCH 16

Question: What massacre began on this day in 1968 in a Vietnamese village?

Answer: My Lai Massacre

On March 16, 1968, American soldiers from Charlie Company began the massacre in My Lai, in Quang Ngai Province, Vietnam. Hundreds of unarmed civilians were killed in the ensuing hours. The atrocity sparked global outrage and raised questions about military conduct in the Vietnam War. A military investigation led to the conviction of Lieutenant William L. Calley in 1971, though the case remains controversial. The My Lai Massacre reshaped public opinion about the war and intensified calls for accountability and troop withdrawal.

* * *

MARCH 17

Question: Which spiritual leader fled his homeland on this day in 1959, seeking asylum in India after a Tibetan uprising?

Answer: Dalai Lama

On March 17, 1959, the 14th Dalai Lama fled Tibet, escaping the Chinese crackdown and crossing the Himalayas to seek asylum in India. His escape established a government-in-exile in Dharamsala and transformed Tibetan political life. The exile created a large Tibetan diaspora and a persistent source of international advocacy for Tibet. The event reshaped Sino-Tibetan relations and set the Dalai Lama on a global stage as a spiritual and political leader. Its legacy continues to influence debates about autonomy, religion, and human rights.

* * *

MARCH 18

Question: What revolutionary government began in Paris on this day in 1871 after the Franco-Prussian War?

Answer: Paris Commune

On March 18, 1871, Parisians proclaimed the Paris Commune, a radical experiment in municipal governance. Delegates were elected to oversee neighborhoods and implement worker-controlled initiatives. The commune lasted until late May 1871, when the French army crushed the government. Its ideas influenced socialist and anarchist movements for generations. The suppression left thousands dead and reshaped debates about democracy and central authority.

* * *

MARCH 19

Question: What uprising intensified in Vienna on this day in 1848 as part of the Revolutions of 1848 in the Austrian Empire?

Answer: Vienna uprising

On March 19, 1848, the Vienna uprising intensified as workers and students demanded constitutional reforms, national rights, and liberal representation. Barricades filled the streets as liberal and nationalist aims clashed with imperial authority. The unrest spread across the empire, provoking concessions but also triggering brutal crackdowns. The events highlighted the momentum of the European revolutions in 1848 and the fragility of old regimes. The suppression did not erase the reformist impulse, which continued to influence European politics for decades.

* * *

MARCH 20

Question: What anti-slavery novel was published on this day in 1852?

Answer: Uncle Tom's Cabin

On March 20, 1852, Harriet Beecher Stowe published Uncle Tom's Cabin, a searing portrayal of slavery in the United States. The novel follows the brutal realities of enslaved life and the moral choices of those who own or resist slavery. Its vivid characters and compassionate storytelling galvanized abolitionist sentiment at home and abroad. Publishers rushed to meet demand, and the book quickly became a landmark best-seller. Its impact intensified national debates over slavery and helped set the stage for the Civil War.

MARCH 21

Question: On this day in 1965, which spacewalker completed the first human outside a spacecraft?

Answer: Alexei Leonov

On March 21, 1965, Alexei Leonov became the first person to exit a spacecraft and float in the vacuum of space during the Voskhod 2 mission. The spacewalk lasted about 12 minutes, and Leonov's suit ballooned, challenging him to squeeze back into the airlock. The daring maneuver demonstrated that humans could operate outside their vehicles, a milestone for spacewalking, docking, and satellite repair. It also exposed design limits in early suits and life-support, pushing engineers to improve reliability for future long-duration missions.

* * *

MARCH 22

Question: On this day in 1622, which English settlement in Virginia was attacked by the Powhatan Confederacy?

Answer: Jamestown

On March 22, 1622, the Powhatan Confederacy launched a coordinated surprise attack on the English settlement at Jamestown, Virginia. The assault killed hundreds of colonists and wounded many more, shattering the fragile frontier outpost. The massacre triggered a brutal cycle of retaliation and led to years of heightened conflict between English settlers and Native peoples. The event underscored the deadly costs of competition for land and resources in early colonial America.

* * *

MARCH 23

Question: On this day in 1775, which American orator delivered the famous 'Give me liberty, or give me death!' speech at the Virginia Convention?

Answer: Patrick Henry

On March 23, 1775, Patrick Henry delivered the fiery call for independence to the Virginia Convention. His words helped mobilize colonists in the brinksmanship against British rule and are often cited as a spark for the American Revolution. The speech reflected a fearlessness about what the colonists might lose—or gain—by choosing resistance. Henry's rhetoric is remembered as a turning point that energized a broader push toward liberty.

* * *

MARCH 24

Question: On this day in 1989, which tanker ran aground in Alaska, triggering a massive oil spill?

Answer: Exxon Valdez

On March 24, 1989, Exxon Valdez struck a reef in Prince William Sound, spilling millions of gallons of crude oil into pristine waters. The disaster devastated marine life, damaged fisheries, and polluted thousands of miles of coastline. Cleanup efforts stretched for years and led to significant changes in oil transportation and spill response policies. The Exxon Valdez disaster remains a benchmark for environmental risk and corporate accountability.

* * *

MARCH 25

Question: On this day in 1807, which Act passed by the British Parliament banned the slave trade within the empire?

Answer: Abolition of the Slave Trade

On March 25, 1807, Britain enacted the Act for the Abolition of the Slave Trade. The measure ended the legal trafficking of enslaved people within the British Empire, a landmark victory for abolitionists. Slavery itself persisted in British colonies for decades afterward, but the act helped catalyze a global movement toward emancipation. The law also pressured other nations to rethink their own slave-trading practices and inspired abolitionist campaigns worldwide.

* * *

MARCH 26

Question: On this day in 1971, which region declared independence from Pakistan, sparking a war that led to the creation of a new nation?

Answer: Bangladesh

On March 26, 1971, Bangladesh declared independence from Pakistan after a brutal crackdown in East Pakistan sparked a full-scale struggle for self-determination. The conflict drew in India and the war lasted for months, ending with the birth of a sovereign nation on December 16, 1971. The new state faced humanitarian crises, refugees, and the daunting task of rebuilding. Bangladesh's emergence reshaped South Asian politics and highlighted the human costs of division and civil conflict. The country remains a testament to resilience and the power of collective self-determination.

* * *

MARCH 27

Question: On this day in 1836, which massacre occurred after Texan prisoners surrendered at Coleto Creek and were executed by Mexican forces?

Answer: Goliad Massacre

On March 27, 1836, the Goliad Massacre unfolded as Mexican forces executed hundreds of Texan prisoners after surrendering at Coleto Creek. Nearly the entire garrison at

Presidio La Bahía was killed, sending shockwaves through the Texan cause. Coming on the heels of the Alamo, the massacre spurred Texan leaders to double down on their fight for independence. The episode also highlighted the brutal realities of the Texas Revolution and influenced later military decisions.

* * *

MARCH 28

Question: On this day in 1979, which nuclear plant experienced a partial meltdown in Pennsylvania?

Answer: Three Mile Island

On March 28, 1979, a partial meltdown occurred at the Three Mile Island Nuclear Generating Station near Harrisburg, Pennsylvania. A combination of equipment failures, design flaws, and human error kicked off a crisis that came dangerously close to a major disaster. It shook public confidence in nuclear power and led to major reforms in reactor operator training and safety protocols. In the decades since, the incident has remained a touchstone in energy policy debates and risk communication.

* * *

MARCH 29

Question: On this day in 1973, which conflict saw its last U.S. combat troops depart?

Answer: Vietnam War

On March 29, 1973, the last U.S. combat troops departed Vietnam under the terms of the Paris Peace Accords. Withdrawal marked the end of American ground involvement, though fighting continued between North and South Vietnam. The withdrawal paved the way for the fall of Saigon in 1975 and the reunification of Vietnam under a single government. Decades later, the war's legacy—trauma, political controversy, and profound cultural shifts—continues to shape American memory.

MARCH 30

Question: On this day in 1867, which territory did the United States purchase from Russia?

Answer: Alaska

On March 30, 1867, the United States completed the purchase of Alaska from Russia for $7.2 million. Many observers called it 'Seward's Folly' at the time, doubting the value of a distant ice-clad land. But the deal quickly paid off as explorers and prospectors uncovered vast resources, including timber, minerals, and eventually oil. The purchase more than doubled the size of the United States and established a strategic gateway to the Arctic.

MARCH 31

Question: What iconic iron lattice tower in Paris opened to the public on this day in 1889?

Answer: Eiffel Tower

On March 31, 1889, the Eiffel Tower opened to the public as the centerpiece of the Exposition Universelle in Paris. Built to showcase iron-age progress, the tower rose about 300 meters tall, a record that stood for decades. Critics dismissed it as an eyesore, while engineers celebrated its daring use of metal and its elegant silhouette. Over time it became a global symbol of Paris and a magnet for visitors, eventually serving as a vital radio and television transmission hub.

4

APRIL

April 1

Question: On this day in 1957, which classic BBC Panorama segment depicted Swiss farmers harvesting spaghetti from trees?

Answer: Spaghetti Tree Hoax

On April 1, 1957, the BBC's Panorama aired a segment about Swiss farmers harvesting spaghetti from trees. This playful hoax tricked many viewers into believing the claim was true. The clever prank exposed how television could shape belief and sparked early discussions about media literacy. Despite being a prank, it left a lasting cultural imprint and is still cited as one of television's most famous hoaxes. Today, it's a reminder to verify evidence and question sensational claims in an age of instant information.

April 2

Question: On this day in 1982, which country invaded the Falkland Islands, triggering a war with the United Kingdom?

Answer: Argentina

On April 2, 1982, Argentina invaded the Falkland Islands, beginning a conflict with the United Kingdom. The Argentine government claimed the islands as part of its territory and sought to assert sovereignty by force. Britain responded with a naval and ground campaign that eventually expelled Argentine forces. The war had profound political and strategic consequences for both nations and reshaped defense policies in the subsequent years. It ended in June 1982 with a British victory and a lingering legacy in the South Atlantic.

* * *

April 3

Question: On this day in 1860, what mail service began its cross-continent run with riders from Missouri to California?

Answer: Pony Express

On April 3, 1860, the Pony Express began its cross-continent run from Missouri to California. Mounted riders and relay stations carried mail across the expanding American frontier in a dramatic, perilous journey. Its bold enterprise slashed travel time for letters and symbolized the race to connect the East and West before telegraph lines captured the route. Although short-lived, lasting about 18 months, it accelerated communications and helped spur the expansion of the

United States. The Pony Express era faded once telegraph networks finally linked the coasts.

* * *

APRIL 4

Question: On this day in 1968, which civil rights leader was assassinated in Memphis?

Answer: Martin Luther King Jr.

On April 4, 1968, Martin Luther King Jr. was assassinated in Memphis, Tennessee. His death sent shockwaves through the American civil rights movement and the nation at large. Riots erupted in many cities as mourners reflected on his leadership and nonviolent philosophy. The events of that week helped catalyze ongoing efforts toward civil rights legislation and social reform. King's legacy continues to inspire movements for racial justice and equality around the world.

* * *

APRIL 5

Question: On this day in 1614, which Native American woman married English settler John Rolfe in Jamestown, Virginia?

Answer: Pocahontas

On April 5, 1614, Pocahontas married English settler John Rolfe in Jamestown, Virginia. This union helped lay the groundwork for a period of relative peace between the

Powhatan Confederacy and the colonists. It facilitated a degree of intercultural exchange and trade that shaped the colony's early years. Pocahontas later traveled to England, where her life contributed to mythic depictions of Native Americans in early American history. Her story remains a focal point in discussions about Native-settler relations in North America.

* * *

APRIL 6

Question: On this day in 1862, which Civil War battle began in Southwestern Tennessee and would last two days?

Answer: Shiloh

On April 6, 1862, the Battle of Shiloh opened in southwestern Tennessee. The clash between Union and Confederate forces shattered prewar assumptions about casualties and set a brutal tempo for the war ahead. Union commanders Grant and Sherman pressed to control critical river corridors, while Confederate leadership faced the steep cost of a decisive defeat on their doorstep. The fighting produced a grim tally of casualties and reshaped military strategies for the remainder of the conflict. Shiloh's ferocity helped accelerate the Union's push toward the Mississippi and redefined how the two sides would wage war.

* * *

APRIL 7

Question: On this day in 1948, which international organization was established to combat global health threats?

Answer: World Health Organization

On April 7, 1948, the World Health Organization was established to coordinate international health efforts. Born from a postwar consensus that health is a universal right, the WHO set out to combat infectious disease, standardize health practices, and respond to emergencies. Its early campaigns tackled malaria, tuberculosis, and smallpox, laying the groundwork for a more connected global health landscape. Over the decades, the organization has expanded into a central hub for health data, policy guidance, and crisis response. The WHO's ongoing work continues to influence public health strategies around the world.

* * *

APRIL **8**

Question: On this day in 1513, which explorer is credited with landing on the coast of Florida while searching for the Fountain of Youth?

Answer: Ponce de León

On April 8, 1513, Spanish explorer Ponce de León is popularly said to have landed on the coast of what is now Florida while pursuing a legendary Fountain of Youth. His voyage marked an important moment in the era of early European exploration of North America and established footholds for later Spanish ventures in the Southeast. The precise details of the landing are debated, but the encounter helped ignite enduring stories about exploration, conquest, and the shaping of colonial maps. The Captain's voyage and claimed discovery fed into centuries of myths and curiosity about the region. Today, Ponce de León's Florida encounter remains a cornerstone tale of the Age of Exploration.

* * *

APRIL 9

Question: On this day in 1865, which event signaled the effective end of the American Civil War?

Answer: Surrender at Appomattox

On April 9, 1865, General Robert E. Lee surrendered to General Ulysses S. Grant at Appomattox Court House, effectively signaling the end of the Civil War. News of the surrender rippled across both Union and Confederacy, offering a symbolic conclusion to four brutal years of fighting. While some Confederate units continued to surrender over the following weeks, the Confederate government was rendered unable to continue armed resistance. The surrender reshaped the national mood, paving the way for Reconstruction and a long, difficult process of reunification. It remains a defining milestone in American memory.

* * *

APRIL 10

Question: On this day in 1912, which ship began its maiden voyage from Southampton to New York?

Answer: Titanic

On April 10, 1912, the RMS Titanic set out from Southampton on its highly anticipated maiden voyage to New York. The grand ocean liner was celebrated as the pinnacle of early 20th-century engineering and luxury. Barely a week into the journey, it struck an iceberg in the North Atlantic, leading to one of the most infamous maritime disasters in history. The tragedy prompted sweeping improvements in maritime safety, including lifeboat requirements and international rescue protocols. The Titanic's story has since become a potent reminder of human hubris, technological ambition, and the fragility of life at sea.

* * *

APRIL 11

Question: Which NASA mission launched on this day in 1970 and later endured a life-threatening in-space crisis but returned safely to Earth?

Answer: Apollo 13

On April 11, 1970, NASA launched Apollo 13 toward the Moon. An oxygen tank explosion crippled the spacecraft, forcing an abort of the lunar landing. The crew and mission control improvised solutions to keep the astronauts safe and bring the ship home. The famous line, "Houston, we have a problem," became a cultural catchphrase for crisis management and teamwork under pressure. In the end, Apollo 13's failure became a triumph of ingenuity and caution that reshaped flight safety.

* * *

APRIL 12

Question: Who became the first human to travel into space aboard Vostok 1?

Answer: Yuri Gagarin

On April 12, 1961, Yuri Gagarin became the first human to travel into space aboard Vostok 1. His single orbit around Earth lasted about 108 minutes and marked the dawn of human spaceflight. The mission demonstrated the feasibility of human spaceflight during the early Cold War era. Gagarin's calm demeanor during the flight and re-entry helped propel space exploration into a new era. The achievement inspired new generations of explorers and shaped future Soviet and international space programs.

* * *

APRIL 13

Question: What massacre occurred on this day in 1919 in Amritsar?

Answer: Jallianwala Bagh massacre

On April 13, 1919, British troops opened fire on a peaceful gathering in Amritsar at Jallianwala Bagh. Hundreds of civilians were killed or wounded in a brutal crackdown that shocked the world. The massacre intensified Indian calls for independence and sparked a reevaluation of British policy. Its memory fuels debates about colonialism, civil rights, and the moral responsibilities of empire. Scholars and communities continue to study its impact as a turning point in the Indian freedom movement.

* * *

April 14

Question: What ship struck an iceberg on this day in 1912?

Answer: Titanic

On April 14, 1912, the passenger liner Titanic struck an iceberg in the frigid North Atlantic. As disaster unfolded, lifeboat shortages and navigational missteps compounded the tragedy. More than 1,500 people perished, making it one of the deadliest peacetime maritime disasters. The catastrophe spurred reforms in maritime safety, including lifeboat requirements and international distress signaling. The Titanic's story endures as a stark cautionary tale about hubris, technology, and human resilience.

* * *

April 15

Question: Who was born on this day in 1452 and would become a Renaissance master?

Answer: Leonardo da Vinci

On April 15, 1452, Leonardo da Vinci was born in Vinci, Italy. He would grow into a towering Renaissance figure, excelling in painting, science, engineering, and anatomy. His notebooks reveal a relentless curiosity and a habit of merging art with invention. Masterpieces like the Mona Lisa and The Last Supper remain enduring testaments to his genius. Da Vinci's multidisciplinary approach helped define the era's spirit of inquiry and innovation.

* * *

APRIL 16

Question: On this day in 1963, which influential letter did Martin Luther King Jr. write while jailed in Birmingham?

Answer: Letter from Birmingham Jail

On April 16, 1963, Martin Luther King Jr. wrote the Letter from Birmingham Jail while imprisoned by local authorities. In it, he addressed white clergy's criticisms and outlined a moral framework for civil disobedience against unjust laws. He argued that injustice anywhere is a threat to justice everywhere and called for nonviolent resistance. The letter helped galvanize the civil rights movement and highlighted the moral urgency of ending segregation.

* * *

APRIL 17

Question: On this day in 1961, which failed invasion began at Cuba's Bay of Pigs?

Answer: Bay of Pigs Invasion

On April 17, 1961, thousands of Cuban exiles backed by the U.S. CIA landed at the Bay of Pigs. The mission aimed to spark a popular uprising against Fidel Castro. The operation was poorly planned and quickly overwhelmed by Cuban forces. The embarrassment strengthened Castro's regime and intensified Cold War tensions between the United States and Cuba.

* * *

APRIL 18

Question: On this day in 1906, which natural disaster struck San Francisco?

Answer: San Francisco earthquake

On April 18, 1906, a devastating earthquake, estimated at magnitude 7.9, struck San Francisco. The quake triggered massive fires that razed large portions of the city. The disaster killed thousands and left many more homeless, reshaping the region's urban landscape. In the aftermath, new building codes and seismic safety measures helped modernize city planning.

* * *

April **19**

Question: On this day in 1775, which battles opened the American Revolutionary War?

Answer: Battles of Lexington and Concord

On April 19, 1775, the Battles of Lexington and Concord began the American Revolutionary War. British troops clashed with colonial militia in Lexington and marched on to Concord, where more fighting followed. These confrontations signaled the start of the broader war for independence. The day became a defining moment in the birth of the United States.

* * *

April **20**

Question: On this day in 1999, which Colorado school experienced a mass shooting?

Answer: Columbine High School massacre

On April 20, 1999, two students carried out a mass shooting at Columbine High School in Colorado. The attack killed 13 people and wounded 24 before the shooters took their own lives. The tragedy triggered a national reckoning on school safety, gun policy, and mental health resources. It remains a watershed moment in late-20th-century American history.

* * *

April 21

Question: On this day in ancient history, who is traditionally credited with founding Rome?

Answer: Romulus

On April 21, 753 BC, Romulus is traditionally credited with founding Rome. The date marks the mythic origins of a city that would become the heart of a vast empire. Roman legends blend divine favor, political ambition, and early struggles between rival factions. Rome's institutions—senate, consuls, and law—would shape governance for centuries. The founding story set a bold, if contentious, template for what Rome would become.

*** * ***

April 22

Question: On this day during the Age of Exploration, which explorer claimed Brazil for Portugal after discovering it?

Answer: Pedro Cabral

On April 22, 1500, Portuguese navigator Pedro Álvares Cabral landed on the coast of what would become Brazil and claimed the land for Portugal. His voyage departed from Portugal with the broader goal of reaching India by sea. The claim opened centuries of Portuguese presence and colonization in South America. Brazil would eventually become the world's largest Portuguese-speaking nation and a cornerstone of global trade networks. Cabral's discovery reshaped maps and power dynamics in the Atlantic world.

* * *

April 23

Question: On this day, which famous playwright's death is commemorated in literary history?

Answer: William Shakespeare

On April 23, 1616, William Shakespeare died in Stratford-upon-Avon. He had left behind a prodigious body of plays, sonnets, and poems that would influence language and storytelling for centuries. Shakespeare's works explore human folly, ambition, love, and tragedy with unrivaled breadth. His enduring influence makes his name synonymous with English literature. The day is observed by scholars and fans as a moment to reflect on his legacy.

* * *

April 24

Question: On this day in Irish history, what uprising began during Easter Week?

Answer: Easter Rising

On April 24, 1916, the Easter Rising began in Dublin as Irish republicans boldly declared independence from British rule. The rebels seized key buildings and proclaimed a new Irish Republic. Although the rebellion was suppressed after about a week, it shifted public opinion and intensified the drive toward independence. The Rising reshaped Ireland's path to sovereignty and left a lasting imprint on Irish identity and commemorations. The event is remembered each year on Easter Monday in many parts of Ireland.

* * *

APRIL 25

Question: On this day in World War I history, which campaign began with landings at Gallipoli?

Answer: Gallipoli Campaign

On April 25, 1915, Allied forces landed on the Gallipoli Peninsula in an attempt to secure a sea route to Russia. This marked the opening phase of the Gallipoli Campaign during World War I. The campaign proved costly and brutal, with high casualties on both sides and difficult terrain. It became a defining episode for Australia and New Zealand, whose soldiers—ANZACs—are remembered for their endurance. The campaign's eventual failure influenced military strategy and national memory for decades.

* * *

APRIL 26

Question: On this day in 1986, which catastrophic nuclear accident began at a power plant in what was then the Ukrainian SSR?

Answer: Chernobyl disaster

On April 26, 1986, the No. 4 reactor at the Chernobyl Nuclear Power Plant exploded during a late-night safety test. The blast released plumes of radioactive material across

Europe and beyond. Operators initially underestimated the severity, delaying containment and evacuation decisions. The disaster triggered long-term health concerns, evacuation of Pripyat, and sweeping reforms in nuclear safety worldwide.

* * *

APRIL 27

Question: On this day in 1521, which Portuguese explorer was killed in the Philippines?

Answer: Ferdinand Magellan

On April 27, 1521, Magellan was killed during the Battle of Mactan in the Philippines, far from his native Portugal. His death occurred while he led the expedition seeking a westward route to Asia. Despite his death, his crew continued the voyage and completed the first circumnavigation of the globe under Elcano. The voyage proved the Earth is round and changed European assumptions about Asia's geography. The expedition's legacy reshaped global trade routes and inspired later explorers.

APRIL 28

Question: On this day in 1789, what event occurred on the HMS Bounty, sparking a famous mutiny?

Answer: Mutiny on the Bounty

On April 28, 1789, tensions aboard the HMS Bounty boiled over as mutineers seized the ship in Tahiti's harbor. Fletcher Christian led the group that overpowered Captain William Bligh and cast him and loyal crew into a small boat. Bligh's remarkable open-boat voyage to safety demonstrated extraordinary navigational skill and endurance. The mutiny became one of the most enduring maritime legends, inspiring books and films and prompting naval reforms. The tale also raises questions about leadership, loyalty, and the costs of exploration.

* * *

APRIL 29

Question: On this day in 1994, what event concluded South Africa's first multiracial elections?

Answer: South Africa's 1994 elections

On April 29, 1994, South Africa's first multiracial democratic elections concluded after three days of voting. The polls delivered a landmark victory for Nelson Mandela and the African National Congress, accelerating the end of apartheid. Mandela would be inaugurated as president in May, symbolizing a nationwide healing process. The vote showcased the power of negotiated transition, international support, and citizen participation. Its legacy continues to shape South Africa's politics, society, and reconciliation efforts.

* * *

APRIL 30

Question: On this day in 1803, what treaty doubled the size of the United States?

Answer: Louisiana Purchase

On April 30, 1803, the Louisiana Purchase treaty was signed by the United States and France. The deal transferred about 827,000 square miles of territory for $15 million, roughly doubling the young nation's size. It opened vast tracts for exploration, paving the way for the Lewis and Clark expedition. The acquisition reshaped North American geography and geopolitics for generations.

5

MAY

May 1

Question: On this day in 1707, what political union created a single kingdom by merging the parliaments of England and Scotland?

Answer: Acts of Union

On May 1st, 1707, the Acts of Union took effect, uniting the Kingdom of England (which already included Wales) and the Kingdom of Scotland into Great Britain. The deal created one Parliament at Westminster and standardized trade and succession rules across the new state. Supporters argued it would bring stability and economic opportunity, while critics in Scotland viewed it as a loss of sovereignty. The union reshaped British politics and set the stage for the rise of the British Empire—while debates over Scottish self-rule continue to echo today.

* * *

MAY 2

Question: On this day in 1933, which German labor organization was dismantled as the Nazis replaced independent unions with a single state-controlled body?

Answer: Trade unions

On May 2nd, 1933, Nazi storm troopers seized union offices across Germany and dismantled the country's independent trade unions. Union leaders were arrested, assets were confiscated, and workers were pressured into joining the Nazi-run German Labour Front (DAF). By crushing organized labor, the regime removed a major source of opposition and tightened control over wages, working conditions, and political life. It was a key step in turning Germany into a one-party dictatorship where civil society institutions were absorbed or destroyed.

* * *

MAY 3

Question: On this day in 1979, which conservative leader became the United Kingdom's first female prime minister after a landmark general election victory?

Answer: Margaret Thatcher

On May 3rd, 1979, Margaret Thatcher led the Conservatives to victory and became Britain's first woman prime minister. She entered office amid high inflation, labor unrest, and a sluggish economy, promising a sharp turn toward free-market policies. Her government's privatizations and battles with trade unions transformed

Britain's economic and political landscape. Admired by supporters and fiercely criticized by opponents, "Thatcherism" remains one of the most debated legacies in modern UK history.

* * *

MAY 4

Question: On this day in 1970, what tragedy occurred at a U.S. university when National Guardsmen opened fire during an antiwar protest?

Answer: Kent State shootings

On May 4th, 1970, the Kent State shootings shocked the United States when Ohio National Guardsmen fired on students protesting the Vietnam War. Four students were killed and nine were wounded, turning a campus demonstration into a national trauma. The event triggered massive student strikes, closing hundreds of colleges and intensifying public debate over the war and civil liberties. Images and stories from Kent State became enduring symbols of a country deeply divided.

* * *

MAY 5

Question: On this day in 1961, which American astronaut became the first U.S. citizen to travel into space aboard Freedom 7?

Answer: Alan Shepard

On May 5th, 1961, Alan Shepard rode the Mercury-Redstone 3 mission—Freedom 7—becoming the first American in space. His suborbital flight lasted about 15 minutes, a rapid but crucial demonstration that the U.S. could put a human atop a rocket and bring him back safely. Coming just weeks after Yuri Gagarin's orbital flight, Shepard's mission boosted American morale and momentum in the Space Race. It helped pave the way for John Glenn's orbit and, ultimately, the Apollo moon landings.

* * *

MAY 6

Question: Who was crowned King of England on this day in 1536 after the execution of Anne Boleyn, marking the start of a dramatic new chapter in the Tudor court?

Answer: Jane Seymour

On May 6th, 1536, Jane Seymour was crowned Queen of England, just days after Anne Boleyn's downfall. Henry VIII moved quickly—both emotionally and politically—seeking a new wife who might finally provide a legitimate male heir. Seymour's rise signaled a shift in court factions, with her family and allies gaining sudden influence. She would give birth to the long-awaited son, Edward VI, but died shortly after childbirth, making her reign brief yet historically pivotal.

* * *

MAY 7

Question: Which unexpected German demand triggered Britain's declaration of war on Germany on this day in 1915, helping widen the First World War's front lines?

Answer: Belgian neutrality

On May 7th, 1915, Britain formally declared war on Germany after Germany demanded that Belgium allow German troops passage—an ultimatum that Belgium refused. Britain had pledged to defend Belgian neutrality under the 1839 Treaty of London, and the violation became a moral and diplomatic rallying point. The move helped frame the conflict as more than a struggle between great powers—it was also about the rights of smaller nations. The decision locked Britain into a major continental war that would reshape Europe and its empires.

* * *

MAY 8

Question: What global health organization was officially established on this day in 1948 to coordinate international responses to disease and public health crises?

Answer: World Health Organization (WHO)

On May 8th, 1948, the World Health Organization (WHO) was established as a specialized agency of the United Nations. Its mission was ambitious: to promote health worldwide and coordinate efforts against threats that ignore borders, from malaria to smallpox. Over time, the WHO helped drive landmark campaigns, including the eradication of smallpox and expanded vaccination programs. It remains a central, often-debated player in global health policy, outbreak response, and setting international medical standards.

MAY 9

Question: Which U.S. president issued the proclamation on this day in 1865 that effectively ended the American Civil War by declaring armed resistance at an end in most Confederate states?

Answer: Andrew Johnson

On May 9th, 1865, President Andrew Johnson issued a proclamation declaring that armed resistance to the United States had largely ended in key Confederate states. Coming after Robert E. Lee's surrender at Appomattox, it was a political signal that the war's organized fighting was essentially over. The proclamation also set the stage for Reconstruction by outlining how regions might return to civil governance. Even so, surrender and demobilization unfolded unevenly, and the deeper battles over rights and power were only beginning.

* * *

MAY 10

Question: What transcontinental engineering feat was completed on this day in 1869 when two railroad lines met in Utah, symbolically uniting the United States by rail?

Answer: The First Transcontinental Railroad

On May 10th, 1869, the First Transcontinental Railroad was completed at Promontory Summit, Utah, when the Union Pacific and Central Pacific lines met. The famous "Golden Spike" ceremony celebrated a technological triumph that cut coast-to-coast travel from months to about a week. It accelerated trade, migration, and the growth of new towns—while also intensifying displacement and hardship for many Indigenous nations. The railroad became a defining engine of America's industrial expansion and a powerful symbol of a rapidly shrinking continent.

* * *

MAY 11

Question: On this day in 330, what city was officially dedicated as the new capital of the Roman Empire, reshaping the empire's future toward the east?

Answer: Constantinople

On May 11, 330, Constantine the Great formally dedicated Constantinople (modern Istanbul) as the Roman Empire's new capital. Strategically positioned on the Bosporus, it controlled key trade routes between Europe and Asia and was easier to defend than Rome. The move accelerated the cultural and political shift that historians often describe as the rise of the Byzantine Empire. For the next thousand years, Constantinople would be a powerhouse of Christianity, commerce, and imperial politics—until its fall in 1453.

* * *

MAY 12

Question: On this day in 1780, what eerie daytime phenomenon plunged parts of New England into near-total darkness, spooking residents who feared the end times?

Answer: The Dark Day

On May 12, 1780, the "Dark Day" settled over New England, turning midday into a gloomy, candlelit night in many towns. People reported ash-like soot, a strange yellow tint to the sky, and animals behaving as if evening had arrived. The leading explanation points to a dense combination of smoke from large forest fires, thick cloud cover, and possibly fog that scattered and blocked sunlight. The episode became a legendary slice of early American history—part science mystery, part cultural flashpoint about fear and faith.

* * *

MAY 13

Question: On this day in 1846, which nation formally declared war on the United States, escalating a border dispute into a full-scale conflict?

Answer: Mexico

On May 13, 1846, Mexico declared war on the United States after mounting tensions and clashes near the Rio Grande. The conflict, known as the Mexican–American War, was fueled by disputes over Texas and the U.S. push toward westward expansion. It ended with the 1848 Treaty of Guadalupe Hidalgo, which transferred a vast swath of territory to the United States, including lands that would become California, Nevada, Utah, and parts of several other states. The war also intensified debates over slavery's expansion—helping set the stage for the American Civil War.

* * *

May 14

Question: On this day in 1610, which French king was assassinated in Paris, abruptly altering the balance of power in Europe?

Answer: Henry IV

On May 14, 1610, King Henry IV of France was assassinated in Paris by François Ravaillac, a Catholic fanatic. Henry had ended decades of French religious conflict with the Edict of Nantes, granting limited toleration to Protestants and stabilizing the kingdom. His death threw France into political uncertainty, leaving his young son Louis XIII on the throne under a regency. The assassination echoed across Europe, shifting alliances and momentum during an era of intense religious and dynastic rivalry.

* * *

MAY 15

Question: On this day in 1974, which country detonated its first nuclear device in a test it described as a "peaceful nuclear explosion"?

Answer: India

On May 15, 1974, India conducted its first nuclear test, code-named "Smiling Buddha," at Pokhran in the Rajasthan desert. Indian officials characterized it as a "peaceful nuclear explosion," but the test signaled a major strategic shift in Asia's security landscape. It triggered international concern and helped spur tighter controls on nuclear technology transfers, including the strengthening of nonproliferation regimes. The test also set the stage for later nuclear developments in South Asia, with enduring effects on regional diplomacy and deterrence.

* * *

MAY 16

Question: On this day in 1929, what gold-domed landmark opened in Hollywood, quickly becoming a symbol of movie premieres and showbiz spectacle?

Answer: Grauman's Chinese Theatre

On May 16, 1929, Grauman's Chinese Theatre opened in Hollywood with a star-studded premiere that helped cement Los Angeles as the capital of American film. Built by showman Sid Grauman, it leaned hard into fantasy architecture to make moviegoing feel like an event. The theatre became famous for its celebrity handprints and footprints set into the forecourt, turning stardom into a public, tactile tradition. Over decades it hosted major premieres and cultural moments, becoming one of the most recognizable cinemas on Earth. Even in the streaming era, it remains a shrine to the idea of Hollywood glamour.

* * *

May 17

Question: On this day in 1954, which U.S. Supreme Court decision declared racial segregation in public schools unconstitutional?

Answer: Brown v. Board of Education

On May 17, 1954, the Supreme Court issued its unanimous decision in Brown v. Board of Education, overturning the "separate but equal" logic that had justified segregated schooling. Chief Justice Earl Warren wrote that separate educational facilities are inherently unequal, a direct blow to Jim Crow. The ruling didn't instantly integrate schools, but it gave the civil rights movement a powerful legal and moral foundation. Follow-up decisions and federal enforcement battles showed how hard equality would be to implement in practice. Brown became a landmark in constitutional law and a turning point in modern American history.

MAY 18

Question: On this day in 1804, which European leader proclaimed himself "Emperor of the French," setting the stage for a continental showdown?

Answer: Napoleon Bonaparte

On May 18, 1804, Napoleon Bonaparte was proclaimed Emperor of the French, transforming the French Republic's revolutionary experiment into an empire under one man's rule. The move aimed to stabilize France after years of upheaval while legitimizing Napoleon's authority at home and abroad. It alarmed Europe's monarchies and accelerated the coalition wars that would define the era. Napoleon's reign reshaped legal systems, warfare, and borders across the continent, even where his armies ultimately failed. His imperial pivot still sparks debate: savior of order or betrayer of the revolution?

* * *

MAY 19

Question: On this day in 1536, which English queen—accused of adultery and treason—was executed in the Tower of London?

Answer: Anne Boleyn

On May 19, 1536, Anne Boleyn was executed at the Tower of London, one of the most dramatic falls from power in Tudor England. Her marriage to Henry VIII had helped trigger England's break with Rome, but court politics and the king's desperation for a male heir turned lethal. Tried on charges widely viewed by historians as dubious, she was beheaded by a skilled swordsman brought from France. Within days, Henry married Jane Seymour, underscoring how quickly the royal narrative could change. Anne's legacy lived on through her daughter, the future Elizabeth I.

* * *

MAY 20

Question: On this day in 1873, which denim-clad garment—created to withstand hard labor—received a U.S. patent and went on to become a global fashion staple?

Answer: Blue jeans

On May 20, 1873, a U.S. patent was granted for riveted work pants associated with Levi Strauss and tailor Jacob Davis, a design meant to survive punishing manual labor. The key innovation was copper rivets reinforcing stress points like pockets and seams, solving a real problem for miners and workers. What began as practical gear in the American West evolved into a symbol of youth culture, rebellion, and everyday comfort worldwide. Over time, blue jeans crossed class lines and continents, becoming one of the most recognizable garments in modern history. Few inventions have traveled so far from workshop utility to cultural icon.

* * *

May 21

Question: On this day in 1927, which American aviator completed the first solo nonstop flight across the Atlantic Ocean, landing in Paris after departing New York?

Answer: Charles Lindbergh

On May 21, 1927, Charles Lindbergh landed at Le Bourget Field outside Paris after flying solo nonstop from New York in the Spirit of St. Louis. The 33½-hour journey proved long-distance aviation could be more than a daredevil stunt —it could be practical. Lindbergh instantly became a global celebrity, sparking an aviation boom and accelerating investment in aircraft design and air routes. The feat also reshaped public imagination, making the world feel suddenly smaller and more connected.

May 22

Question: On this day in 1856, which U.S. senator was brutally attacked with a cane on the Senate floor after a speech about "Bleeding Kansas"?

Answer: Charles Sumner

On May 22, 1856, Massachusetts senator Charles Sumner was beaten with a cane by South Carolina representative Preston Brooks inside the U.S. Senate chamber. The assault followed Sumner's fiery anti-slavery speech condemning violence in Kansas and mocking pro-slavery leaders. In the North, Sumner became a symbol of slavery's brutality; in parts of the South, Brooks was celebrated and even sent replacement canes. The incident crystallized sectional hatred and helped push the nation closer to the Civil War.

* * *

MAY 23

Question: On this day in 1934, which infamous outlaws were ambushed and killed by Texas and Louisiana lawmen near Gibsland, Louisiana?

Answer: Bonnie and Clyde

On May 23, 1934, Bonnie Parker and Clyde Barrow were ambushed and killed on a rural road near Gibsland, Louisiana. The pair had become tabloid legends during the Great Depression, glamorized by headlines even as they robbed banks and murdered officers. Their deaths marked a turning point in how law enforcement pursued mobile, heavily armed criminals across state lines. The story's afterlife—books, ballads, and films—helped define America's enduring fascination with outlaw mythology.

* * *

MAY 24

Question: On this day in 1883, which structure opened to the public as the longest suspension bridge in the world, linking Manhattan and Brooklyn?

Answer: The Brooklyn Bridge

On May 24, 1883, the Brooklyn Bridge officially opened, connecting Manhattan and Brooklyn with a then-unprecedented suspension design. Engineered by John A. Roebling and completed under the leadership of Washington Roebling (with crucial help from Emily Warren Roebling), it became a monument to industrial-era ambition. Its success proved that massive steel-cable bridges could be safe and practical, changing urban transportation and city growth. The bridge remains an icon of New York and a symbol of engineering confidence.

MAY 25

Question: On this day in 1977, which film premiered and ignited a global pop-culture phenomenon, introducing audiences to Luke Skywalker and the Force?

Answer: Star Wars

On May 25, 1977, Star Wars premiered and rapidly transformed the movie business into a blockbuster-driven, merchandise-powered engine. George Lucas's space opera blended mythic storytelling with groundbreaking visual effects that raised audience expectations overnight. The film's success reshaped Hollywood marketing, from wide releases to tie-in products and franchise planning. Decades later, it still defines modern fandom and the idea that a film can become a shared cultural universe.

MAY 26

Question: On this day in 1521, which Spanish conquistador began the final siege that would bring down the Aztec capital of Tenochtitlan?

Answer: Hernán Cortés

On May 26, 1521, Hernán Cortés launched the decisive siege of Tenochtitlan, the island capital of the Aztec Empire. With Indigenous allies, Spanish forces cut causeways and used brigantines to control the lake, strangling the city's supplies. After months of brutal fighting, the city fell in August, marking a turning point in the Spanish conquest of Mexico. The collapse reshaped the Americas through colonial rule, demographic catastrophe from disease, and a profound cultural transformation that still reverberates today.

* * *

MAY 27

Question: On this day in 1964, which prime minister was appointed to lead independent India after the death of Jawaharlal Nehru?

Answer: Lal Bahadur Shastri

On May 27, 1964, Lal Bahadur Shastri became India's prime minister, stepping into office after Jawaharlal Nehru's death. Known for his modest lifestyle and steady demeanor, Shastri sought to stabilize the country during a tense Cold War era. His leadership soon faced major tests, including food shortages and the 1965 war with Pakistan. He famously popularized the slogan "Jai Jawan, Jai Kisan," linking national security with agricultural strength.

* * *

MAY 28

Question: On this day in 1937, which British monarch opened the first parliament of his reign, a landmark moment after the abdication crisis?

Answer: King George VI

On May 28, 1937, King George VI opened Parliament for the first time, signaling stability after the upheaval of Edward VIII's abdication. The event came just weeks after George VI's coronation, when the monarchy was working to rebuild public confidence. Despite a severe stammer, the king carried out highly visible duties that helped define his image as conscientious and resilient. His reign would soon be shaped by World War II, when his steadfast presence became a symbol of national endurance.

* * *

MAY 29

Question: On this day in 1953, which two men reached the summit of Mount Everest first, completing the world's most famous mountaineering goal?

Answer: Edmund Hillary and Tenzing Norgay

On May 29, 1953, Edmund Hillary and Tenzing Norgay became the first confirmed climbers to stand atop Mount

Everest. Their ascent was part of a British expedition led by John Hunt, relying on teamwork, careful logistics, and high-altitude oxygen. News of the success electrified the world and became entwined with the era's spirit of exploration. It also elevated Sherpa expertise and labor into global view, even as debates about recognition and credit continued for decades.

* * *

May 30

Question: On this day in 1431, which French heroine was executed in Rouen after being tried for heresy during the Hundred Years' War?

Answer: Joan of Arc

On May 30, 1431, Joan of Arc was burned at the stake in Rouen after a politically charged trial orchestrated by her English enemies and their allies. Captured the previous year, she was accused of heresy and condemned despite her pivotal role in revitalizing French resistance. Her death turned her into a powerful martyr figure, fueling French morale long after her execution. In 1456 her conviction was overturned, and in 1920 she was canonized—cementing her as one of history's most enduring symbols of courage and faith.

* * *

May 31

Question: On this day in 1889, what catastrophic flood—triggered by the failure of a poorly maintained dam—devastated a Pennsylvania industrial town and became one of the deadliest disasters in U.S. history?

Answer: The Johnstown Flood

On May 31, 1889, the South Fork Dam collapsed after days of heavy rain, unleashing a wall of water that tore through Johnstown, Pennsylvania. The torrent carried debris, homes, and even railcars, killing more than 2,200 people in minutes and leaving the town in ruins. A wealthy club that owned the dam faced intense public blame, but survivors struggled to win accountability in court—fueling calls for stronger safety standards. The disaster also showcased the growing role of the American Red Cross, as Clara Barton led one of its first major relief efforts. Johnstown became a turning point in how Americans understood industrial risk, disaster response, and civic responsibility.

6

JUNE

June 1

Question: On this day in 1953, which monarch was crowned in Westminster Abbey?

Answer: Queen Elizabeth II

On June 2, 1953, Queen Elizabeth II was crowned at Westminster Abbey in London after her accession the previous year. Her coronation was a global television event, symbolizing a modernizing monarchy. The ceremony blended ancient pageantry with postwar optimism. Her long reign would shape Britain and the Commonwealth for decades.

* * *

June 2

Question: On this day in 1783, which invention's first public flight took place in Paris, thrilling spectators with a lightweight, non-balloon craft?

Answer: Hot air balloon

On June 4, 1783, the Montgolfier brothers showcased the first public demonstration of a hot-air balloon in Paris. The flight proved that lighter-than-air craft could lift passengers, not just experiments. It opened a new era of human flight and sparked a global fascination with aeronautics. The era of balloons and later airplanes owed a debt to that skyward leap.

* * *

June 3

Question: On this day in 1967, which conflict began after fighting erupted between Israel and several neighboring Arab states?

Answer: Six-Day War

On June 5, 1967, the Six-Day War broke out in the Middle East as Israel faced coordinated attacks from Egypt, Jordan, and Syria. Despite being outnumbered at the start, Israeli forces achieved a rapid and decisive victory, capturing the Sinai Peninsula, West Bank, and Golan Heights. The war dramatically altered the map and geopolitics of the region. Its consequences continue to influence Middle Eastern diplomacy to this day.

* * *

JUNE 4

Question: On this day in 1989, which massive Chinese government crackdown began, ending weeks of pro-democracy protests centered on Tiananmen Square?

Answer: Tiananmen crackdown

On June 4, 1989, Chinese troops and tanks moved into Tiananmen Square to quell protests, ending weeks of demonstrations that called for political reform. The images of tanks and students became a defining moment of late-Cold War era Asia. The crackdown prompted international condemnation and a long period of political tightening within China. The event remains a focal point in discussions of civil liberties and state power.

* * *

JUNE 5

Question: On this day in 1789, which major political event in France began with a dramatic volley that marked the start of a new era?

Answer: Storming of the Bastille

On June 14, 1789, a few days after June 1 is referenced for context, the storming of the Bastille became a powerful symbol of the French Revolution's egalitarian ideals. Though the rebellion's momentum built over weeks, the Bastille's fall became a rallying cry for liberty, equality, and fraternity. It signaled a shift from absolute monarchy toward popular sovereignty and inspired revolutionary movements worldwide.

* * *

JUNE 6

Question: What operation began the Allied invasion of Normandy on this day in 1944?

Answer: Operation Overlord

On June 6, 1944, Allied forces stormed the beaches of Normandy, opening a crucial western front in World War II. The invasion was codenamed Operation Overlord, a massive coordinated assault involving air, sea, and land forces from the United States, Britain, Canada, and other allies. Despite stiff German defenses, the landing established a foothold in occupied Europe and accelerated the push toward Paris. The day is remembered as a turning point that shifted momentum away from the Axis powers. Its success paved the way for the liberation of Western Europe in the months that followed.

* * *

JUNE 7

Question: Which treaty, signed on this day in 1494, divided newly discovered lands outside Europe between Spain and Portugal?

Answer: Treaty of Tordesillas

On June 7, 1494, the Treaty of Tordesillas was signed under papal mediation to resolve competing claims in newly explored territories. A line of demarcation drawn by Pope Alexander VI split the non-European world between Spain and Portugal. The agreement shaped colonial ambitions in the Americas and beyond for centuries. It effectively granted vast western territories to Spain and eastern routes and Africa to Portugal. The treaty's legacy influenced language, culture, and borders long after the explorers' voyages.

* * *

JUNE 8

Question: Which religious leader died on this day in 632 CE, shaping the early Islamic world?

Answer: Prophet Muhammad

On June 8, 632 CE, Prophet Muhammad passed away in Medina after guiding the Muslim community for years. His death left a leadership vacuum that sparked debates about succession and governance. The early caliphate grew out of these deliberations, influencing the political and religious trajectory of Islam. Within a few decades, Muslim armies and scholars helped spread the faith across the Middle East, North Africa, and beyond. Muhammad's teachings and example continued to shape Muslim practice for centuries.

* * *

JUNE 9

Question: Which strategic plateau did Israeli forces capture on this day in 1967 during the Six-Day War?

Answer: Golan Heights

On June 9, 1967, during the Six-Day War, Israeli forces seized the Golan Heights from Syria. The plateau's high ground provided an advantageous military position and access to vital water resources, making its capture a watershed moment in the conflict. The victory reshaped regional security dynamics and became a lasting point of contention in Middle Eastern diplomacy. The battle's outcome contributed to Israel's broader territorial gains in the war and influenced subsequent negotiations and armistice lines.

* * *

June 10

Question: Which war concluded on this day in 1967 after six days of fighting?

Answer: Six-Day War

On June 10, 1967, the Six-Day War effectively ended with a ceasefire brokered after six days of intense fighting. Israel had achieved rapid victories on multiple fronts, capturing territories including the Sinai Peninsula, the West Bank, Gaza Strip, and the Golan Heights. The war's aftermath dramatically altered maps, politics, and security arrangements in the Middle East, leading to decades of diplomacy, conflict, and negotiation. The quick conflict left a lasting imprint on international relations in the region.

JUNE 11

Question: What action did Alabama Governor George Wallace take to block integration at the University of Alabama on this day in 1963?

Answer: Stand in the Schoolhouse Door

On June 11, 1963, George Wallace physically blocked entry to the University of Alabama's law school, attempting to enforce segregation despite a federal court order. The moment became an enduring symbol of resistance to civil rights reform in the United States. Federal authorities ultimately intervened, and the students were admitted, marking a pivotal, though contested, moment in the fight for equality. Wallace's stunt drew national attention and intensified debates about state versus federal power in enforcing desegregation. The event is often cited as a catalyst that helped accelerate federal civil rights action in the 1960s.

* * *

JUNE 12

Question: Which civil rights leader was assassinated in Jackson, Mississippi, on this day in 1963, galvanizing national attention to the movement?

Answer: Medgar Evers

On June 12, 1963, Medgar Evers, the NAACP field secretary for Mississippi, was assassinated in Jackson. His death became a rallying cry for civil rights organizers across the country. Evers had spent his career organizing voter-registration drives and investigating crimes against Black citizens, often under threat of violence. His death underscored the dangers faced by activists and helped galvanize support for landmark civil rights legislation. The case also highlighted the urgent need for federal protection of civil rights workers in the Jim Crow South.

* * *

JUNE 13

Question: On this day in 1775, which military organization did the Continental Congress establish to coordinate the colonial war effort against Britain?

Answer: Continental Army

On June 14, 1775, the Continental Congress formally established the Continental Army to coordinate the colonists' fight against Britain during the American Revolutionary War. George Washington was appointed as its commander-in-chief. The army represented a unifying symbol of colonial resolve and a shift from colonial militias to a centralized, standing force. Its creation helped organize military strategy, supply lines, and recruitment across the growing number of revolutionary settlements. The Continental Army would later play a decisive role in American independence.

* * *

JUNE 14

Question: On this day in 1777, which basic emblem of the new United States was adopted by the Continental Congress, laying the groundwork for a national flag?

Answer: The Stars and Stripes (Flag)

On June 14, 1777, the Continental Congress passed a resolution adopting the stars and stripes as the flag of the United States. The design symbolized the union of the original thirteen colonies and became a powerful national symbol. Over the years, the flag evolved with the addition of more stars as new states joined the Union. The act helped foster a shared identity during the Revolutionary era and into the expansion of the United States. Today, the flag remains a testament to the country's founding ideals and its ongoing evolution.

* * *

June 15

Question: On this day in 1215, which foundational document—limiting royal power and safeguarding certain rights—was sealed, signaling a long-term shift toward the rule of law in England?

Answer: Magna Carta

On June 15, 1215, the Magna Carta was sealed, a charter that limited the powers of the English king and protected the rights of Barons at first, and later broader liberties for subjects. Although initially a peace treaty among the nobility, it became a symbol of the idea that rulers are subject to law. Over the centuries, Magna Carta's legacy influenced the development of due process and constitutional law in the English-speaking world. The document's enduring significance lies in its lasting message: governance should be constrained by rights that protect individuals from arbitrary power.

JUNE 16

Question: On this day in 1815, which battle marked Napoleon Bonaparte's last major victory before Waterloo?

Answer: Battle of Ligny

On June 16, 1815, the Battle of Ligny pitted Napoleon's French army against the Prussian forces near Ligny, Belgium. Napoleon secured a tactical victory, pressing the Prussian army back. However, this success proved pyrrhic as the British and Prussian forces would defeat him at Waterloo two days later. Ligny demonstrated Napoleon's audacious strategic posture even as his empire was nearing its end. The battle's outcome shaped the post-Napoleonic settlement in Europe.

* * *

June 17

Question: On this day in 1789, which body proclaimed itself the National Assembly, sparking the move toward constitutional reform?

Answer: National Assembly

On June 17, 1789, delegates from the Third Estate gathered in defiance of the Estates-General and proclaimed themselves the National Assembly. This bold move signaled a shift in political power toward popular sovereignty and constitutional reform. The act intensified the crisis with King Louis XVI and sparked a broader push for a new constitutional order in France. It laid the groundwork for the drafting of a constitution and the revolutionary reforms to come. In hindsight, it marks a turning point that would shape the French Revolution for years.

* * *

June 18

Question: On this day in 1815, which decisive battle ended Napoleon's rule and altered European politics?

Answer: Battle of Waterloo

On June 18, 1815, the Battle of Waterloo saw Wellington's Allied army decisively defeat Napoleon's forces near Waterloo, Belgium. The loss ended Napoleon's rule as Emperor of the French. It forced the reshaping of Europe's political map at the Congress of Vienna. The term Waterloo has since become a byword for a final, crushing defeat.

Napoleon would be exiled to Saint Helena, ending his bid for European domination.

* * *

JUNE 19

Question: On this day in 1865, which celebration commemorates the emancipation of enslaved people in Texas and became a symbol of freedom across the United States?

Answer: Juneteenth

On June 19, 1865, Union General Gordon Granger arrived in Galveston, Texas and proclaimed freedom for enslaved people there, effectively enforcing the Emancipation Proclamation in the state. Word of emancipation spread slowly, but the day became a symbol of freedom across the United States. The celebration grew into Juneteenth, a day of remembrance and education about African American history and culture. In 2021, Juneteenth became a federal holiday, codifying its importance in national memory. Today, Juneteenth remains a powerful reminder of resilience and ongoing civil rights work.

* * *

JUNE 20

Question: On this day in 1789, which pledge by the Third Estate vowed not to disband until a constitution was written?

Answer: Tennis Court Oath

On June 20, 1789, the representatives of the Third Estate gathered in a Parisian tennis court after being locked out of the Estates-General and took an oath. They vowed not to disband until a constitutional framework was established. The Tennis Court Oath became a powerful symbol of popular sovereignty and the push for constitutional reform. It helped rally support for reforms that accelerated the French Revolution. The event is remembered as a cornerstone moment in the story of liberty and democracy.

* * *

JUNE 21

Question: What state became the ninth to ratify the U.S. Constitution on this day in 1788?

Answer: New Hampshire

On June 21, 1788, New Hampshire became the ninth state to ratify the United States Constitution, sealing the document's path to operation. Without New Hampshire's approval, the new framework might have stalled and the union's future uncertain. The ratification highlighted the delicate balance between state sovereignty and a stronger central government. This moment is often cited as the practical birth of the United States government as we know it. Its approval gave confidence to other states that the Constitution could work in a diverse republic.

* * *

June 22

Question: Which astronomer was forced to recant his heliocentric view on this day in 1633?

Answer: Galileo Galilei

On June 22, 1633, Galileo Galilei faced the Roman Inquisition in a formal trial. He was compelled to recant his support for heliocentrism, the idea that Earth orbits the Sun. The proceedings underscored the tense clash between emerging scientific evidence and established ecclesiastical authority. Galileo's sentence placed him under house arrest for the rest of his life, stifling his public scientific work but not erasing his influence. The episode left a lasting imprint on the history of science, signaling the rough road to scientific ideas breaking free from dogma.

* * *

June 23

Question: Which environmental disaster highlighted the need for regulation when the Cuyahoga River caught fire on this day in 1969?

Answer: Cuyahoga River fire

On June 23, 1969, the Cuyahoga River in Cleveland burst into flames after years of industrial pollution. The dramatic image spurred public outrage and helped catalyze the modern environmental movement. Lawmakers soon pushed for stronger pollution controls, culminating in landmark regulations like the Clean Water Act. The event also shifted public perception, turning water pollution into a national political issue. In hindsight, the fire became a symbol of the era's environmental awakening.

* * *

JUNE 24

Question: What major blockade began on this day in 1948 when the Soviet Union blocked West Berlin?

Answer: Berlin Blockade

On June 24, 1948, the Soviet Union began the Berlin Blockade. Western Allies responded with the Berlin Airlift, delivering thousands of tons of supplies by air for nearly a year. The standoff crystallized Cold War tensions and demonstrated how logistics and morale could shape geopolitics. It also led to the creation of the Federal Republic of Germany (West Germany) and reinforced Western alliances like NATO. The blockade's legacy endures as a pivotal moment in 20th-century diplomacy.

* * *

JUNE 25

Question: Which battle began on this day in 1876, pitting U.S. Army troops under General Custer against Lakota, Sioux, and Cheyenne fighters?

Answer: Battle of the Little Bighorn

On June 25, 1876, the Battle of the Little Bighorn began. Custer's 7th Cavalry found itself overwhelmed by a large coalition of Lakota, Sioux, and Cheyenne warriors. The defeat became known as 'Custer's Last Stand' and shocked the American public. In the aftermath, U.S. policy toward the Great Sioux War intensified frontier military efforts. The battle endures in memory as a symbol of Native American resistance and the brutal realities of the American West.

June 26

Question: Which foundational document was signed on this day in 1945 to establish the United Nations?

Answer: UN Charter

On June 26, 1945, delegates from 50 nations gathered in San Francisco to sign a charter that would become the backbone of the postwar international order. The United Nations Charter created the framework for international cooperation, peacekeeping, and human rights that many countries still rely on today. Its creation represented a collective hope to prevent another global conflict on the scale of World War I. The charter also established the UN's main organs, including the General Assembly and the Security Council, and set out the principles of sovereign equality and collective security. This day marked the birth of a new era in international diplomacy and global governance.

* * *

June 27

Question: On this day in 1864, which Civil War battle took place in Georgia, featuring Union forces attempting a costly frontal assault against Confederate defenses?

Answer: Battle of Kennesaw Mountain

On June 27, 1864, the Battle of Kennesaw Mountain opened as Union forces under General William T. Sherman confronted Confederate troops in northwestern Georgia. Despite heavy losses, the battle demonstrated the ferocity of defensive mountain warfare and the challenges of maneuvering a numerically superior army against entrenched positions. Although Sherman would eventually push Confederate forces back, the engagement underscored the grueling nature of the Atlanta Campaign. The battle is often remembered for its brutal artillery fire and stubborn hilltop defenses. It helped set the stage for Sherman's later, more successful operations in the region.

June 28

Question: On this day in 1914, the assassination of which archduke sparked a chain of events that led to World War I?

Answer: Archduke Franz Ferdinand

On June 28, 1914, Archduke Franz Ferdinand of Austria and his wife were assassinated in Sarajevo. The killing by Gavrilo Princip set off a rapid series of diplomatic escalations among European powers, drawing in allies and triggering mobilizations that spiraled into a full-scale war. The conflict reshaped national borders, collapsed empires, and altered the balance of power for a century. The assassination highlighted how a single event in a volatile alliance system could ignite a continental war. It remains a pivotal turning point in modern history.

* * *

JUNE 29

Question: On this day in 1613, which London theatre was destroyed by a fire during a performance, leading to a rapid rebuild?

Answer: Globe Theatre

On June 29, 1613, the Globe Theatre in London caught fire after a misfired theatrical cannon during a performance of Henry VIII. The thatched roof, built from slow-burning timber, burned rapidly, and the building collapsed within hours. Fortunately, most of the cast and audience escaped unharmed, though the disaster prompted a quick rebuild on the same site. The Globe would reopen the following year, and the incident became a legendary anecdote about early modern theatre. The fire also cemented the theatre's place in literary history, given its association with Shakespeare.

* * *

JUNE 30

Question: On this day in 1997, which historic handover occurred, marking the end of British rule over a major Asian territory?

Answer: Hong Kong handover

On June 30, 1997, Britain officially handed over Hong Kong to China, completing the transfer of sovereignty that culminated a century of colonial rule. The handover ceremony symbolized a transition to a 'one country, two systems' framework, intended to preserve Hong Kong's distinctive economic and legal institutions under Chinese governance. The date marks the end of British administration and the beginning of a new phase in Hong Kong's political evolution. The event had lasting global implications for international diplomacy, regional security, and the territories' identities.

7

JULY

July 1

Question: On this day in 1863, which battle began that would become a turning point in the Civil War?

Answer: Battle of Gettysburg

On July 1, 1863, Union and Confederate forces clashed near Gettysburg, Pennsylvania. The three-day battle would become one of the war's bloodiest, drawing tens of thousands of soldiers to the fields. By day three, Union defenses held high ground and repelled Confederate assaults. The Confederate retreat marked a turning point, ending Lee's invasion of the North. Gettysburg would come to symbolize endurance and transformed the war's momentum in favor of the Union.

* * *

July 2

Question: On this day in 1776, what major decision did the Continental Congress approve?

Answer: Independence from Britain

On July 2, 1776, the Continental Congress formally voted to declare independence from Britain. The decision was followed by the drafting of a formal declaration outlining the reasons for separation. Although the Declaration of Independence would be adopted on July 4, the July 2 vote marked the decisive break. The move set in motion the creation of a new nation grounded in Enlightenment principles. July 2–4 became a shorthand for America's birth, celebrated in histories and holidays.

* * *

July 3

Question: On this day in 1863, which Confederate assault marked the climax of the Battle of Gettysburg?

Answer: Pickett's Charge

On July 3, 1863, Pickett's Charge culminated the Battle of Gettysburg. About 12,500 Confederate soldiers marched across open ground toward the center of the Union line. Artillery and rifle fire shredded the assault as Union defenses held firm. The failed charge doomed the Confederate offensive and forced a retreat. Historians view the episode as a turning point that shifted momentum toward Union victory.

* * *

JULY 4

Question: On this day in 1776, which document was adopted by the Continental Congress?

Answer: Declaration of Independence

On July 4, 1776, the Continental Congress adopted the Declaration of Independence. Written primarily by Thomas Jefferson, the document proclaimed the colonies' break from Britain and laid out principles of liberty and rights. It justified revolution by appealing to natural rights and grievances against the Crown. The Declaration became a founding creed of the United States and inspired movements for freedom worldwide. Its legacy endures in American political culture and in global discussions of human rights.

* * *

JULY 5

Question: On this day in 1687, which scientific work by Isaac Newton was published?

Answer: Principia Mathematica

On July 5, 1687, Isaac Newton's Principia Mathematica was published. It laid out the laws of motion and universal gravitation that explained both earthly and celestial phenomena. It connected planetary motion with terrestrial physics and unified the heavens and the Earth under one framework. Its mathematical approach and predictive power catalyzed the Scientific Revolution. The Principia's influence extends through physics, engineering, and science to this day.

* * *

July 6

Question: What milestone did Louis Pasteur achieve on this day in 1885 that changed medicine?

Answer: Rabies vaccine

On July 6, 1885, Louis Pasteur announced the first successful vaccination against rabies in a human. The patient, a boy named Joseph Meister, had been bitten by a rabid dog, and the treatment used Pasteur's weakened-virus approach. The success not only saved Meister but also validated Pasteur's vaccine methods, pushing immunology from theory to practice. The breakthrough spurred rapid advancement in vaccine research and public health thinking worldwide. It marked a turning point in how society protects itself from deadly infectious diseases.

* * *

July 7

Question: What city experienced coordinated suicide bombings on public transit on this day in 2005?

Answer: London

On July 7, 2005, London was hit by a coordinated terrorist attack on the Underground and a bus, killing 52 people. Four attackers carried out the bombings within two hours during the morning rush. The events shook the UK and reverberated around the world, intensifying debates about security and civil liberties. Britain mobilized emergency responses, reviewed anti-terror policies, and heightened vigilance on public spaces. The date is remembered as a grim reminder of modern urban terrorism.

* * *

JULY 8

Question: What term rose to prominence after the Roswell incident reports on this day in 1947?

Answer: Flying saucer

On July 8, 1947, the Roswell Daily Record reported that military personnel had recovered debris from a mysterious object near Roswell, New Mexico. The initial story sparked headlines about a 'flying saucer'—a phrase that captured the public imagination. The Army later clarified the debris was from a weather balloon, but the myth persisted in popular culture. The incident sparked decades of UFO lore and debates about government transparency. It remains one of the most famous 'close encounters' in history.

* * *

JULY 9

Question: Which operation began the Allied invasion of Sicily on this day in 1943?

Answer: Operation Husky

On July 9, 1943, Allied forces launched Operation Husky, the invasion of Sicily, opening a new front in the European theater. Troops landed on the island and fought through a combination of amphibious assaults and inland battles. The campaign forced Axis forces to divert resources from Italy, hastening the downfall of Mussolini's regime. The success boosted Allied confidence and contributed to the momentum that led to the Italian surrender. Sicily's fall also helped set the stage for the Allied invasion of mainland Europe.

* * *

July 10

Question: Which major WWII air campaign began on this day in 1940?

Answer: Battle of Britain

On July 10, 1940, the Battle of Britain opened as the Luftwaffe launched sustained aerial assaults against Britain. The Royal Air Force mounted determined resistance, implementing radar-guided defense and strategic bombing avoidance. The campaign became the first major military campaign fought entirely by air forces, with Britain standing against the threat of a German invasion. Its outcome hinged on air superiority and regional resilience, ultimately preventing a Nazi invasion of the island. The Battle of Britain reshaped WWII strategy and morale on both sides.

* * *

July 11

Question: On this day in 1804, where did the famous duel take place?

Answer: Weehawken

On July 11, 1804, a famous duel took place in Weehawken, New Jersey. Two leading American political figures faced off over a dispute that had become deeply personal and national in scope. Hamilton was mortally wounded and died the next day, a blow to his federalist vision and a turning point in U.S. politics. The duel's aftermath damaged Burr's career and left a lasting stain on the era's political culture.

* * *

July 12

Question: On this day in 1804, who died after the duel?

Answer: Alexander Hamilton

On July 12, 1804, Alexander Hamilton died from wounds suffered the day before in the Weehawken duel. The death marked the end of a towering Federalist voice and a turning point in early American politics. Hamilton's legacy shaped finance, governance, and political integrity for generations. The duel's aftermath damaged Burr's career and left a lasting stigma on political honor.

* * *

JULY 13

Question: On this day in 1985, which global concert helped raise funds for famine relief in Africa?

Answer: Live Aid

On July 13, 1985, Live Aid united musicians across the globe to raise funds for famine relief in Africa. Spearheaded by Bob Geldof and Midge Ure, the twin concerts at Wembley and JFK Stadium drew massive audiences. Televised to hundreds of millions, the event raised significant funds and highlighted the power of large-scale philanthropic events. Live Aid also popularized modern charity concerts and inspired future humanitarian efforts.

* * *

JULY 14

Question: On this day in 1789, which fortress did revolutionaries storm on Bastille Day?

Answer: Bastille

On July 14, 1789, the storming of the Bastille became a potent symbol of the French Revolution. A crowd's action embodied the surge of popular sovereignty that challenged the Ancien Régime. Although the Bastille itself was not crucial militarily by then, its fall carried enormous political significance. Bastille Day has endured as a celebration of liberty and civic action across France.

* * *

July 15

Question: On this day in 1099, which army captured Jerusalem during the First Crusade?

Answer: Crusaders

On July 15, 1099, the Crusaders breached the walls of Jerusalem after weeks of siege. The capture established the Latin Kingdom of Jerusalem and reshaped the region's political landscape. The event intensified Christian–Muslim conflicts in the Middle East for generations. Its memory influenced medieval theology, pilgrimage, and the broader history of the Crusades.

* * *

July 16

Question: On this day in 1945, where did the first detonation of a nuclear device take place?

Answer: Trinity Site

On July 16, 1945, the Trinity test at the White Sands Proving Ground near Alamogordo, New Mexico, marked the first detonation of a nuclear device. The blast produced a brilliant mushroom cloud and energy equivalent to about 20 kilotons of TNT. It was the capstone of the Manhattan Project, a race to harness atomic power for wartime ends. The test reshaped military strategy, international relations, and science, signaling the dawn of the nuclear age. Today, the Trinity Site stands as a historical landmark and a reminder of the profound consequences of scientific breakthroughs.

* * *

JULY 17

Question: On this day in 1955, which American amusement park opened in Anaheim?

Answer: Disneyland

On July 17, 1955, Disneyland opened its gates to the public in Anaheim, California, offering a theme-park experience built around storytelling. The ambitious project, conceived by Walt Disney, blended immersive attractions, live entertainment, and a new consumer-era of family friendliness. The opening day was chaotic but memorable, with heat, crowds, and technical hiccups captured in a televised broadcast. Disneyland's success helped popularize the concept of theme parks as immersive experiences and spurred a global industry of imitators and innovations. Its enduring influence reshaped popular culture and tourism.

* * *

JULY 18

Question: On this day in 64 CE, which city endured a catastrophic fire that destroyed much of it?

Answer: Rome

On July 18, 64 CE, a catastrophic fire broke out in Rome and burned for days, destroying large portions of the city. Ancient historians debated its origins, and Nero's reputation for political maneuvering afterward helped shape its enduring legend. In the aftermath, the Emperor initiated rebuilding efforts and tightened urban regulations to reduce fire risk. Rome's reconstruction changed its skyline, architecture, and social life for generations. The Great Fire remains a defining moment in ancient history and a cautionary tale about urban vulnerability.

* * *

July 19

Question: On this day in 1848, which gathering marked a pivotal moment in the women's rights movement in upstate New York?

Answer: Seneca Falls Convention

On July 19, 1848, the Seneca Falls Convention opened in Seneca Falls, New York, marking the first organized women's rights convention in the United States. Led by Lucretia Mott and Elizabeth Cady Stanton, attendees drafted the Declaration of Sentiments, demanding equal rights, including suffrage. The gathering energized a burgeoning reform movement and laid the groundwork for decades of activism. While it did not immediately grant universal rights, its legacy catalyzed future milestones in the fight for gender equality. The Seneca Falls Convention remains a watershed moment in American democracy.

* * *

July 20

Question: On this day in 1969, which mission successfully landed humans on the Moon?

Answer: Apollo 11

On July 20, 1969, Apollo 11 touched down in the Sea of Tranquility on the Moon. Neil Armstrong and Buzz Aldrin became the first humans to walk on another world, while Michael Collins orbited above. Armstrong's iconic first steps and call, 'That's one small step for man, one giant leap for mankind,' resonated around the globe. The mission symbolized scientific achievement, technological prowess, and a moment of shared wonder across nations. It remains a defining milestone in space exploration and a touchstone of 20th-century history.

* * *

JULY 21

Question: On this day in 1969, who became the first person to walk on the Moon?

Answer: Neil Armstrong

On July 21, 1969, Neil Armstrong became the first person to walk on the Moon. Buzz Aldrin joined him on the lunar surface while Michael Collins orbited above. Armstrong's 'one small step' moment was broadcast to millions around the world and symbolized a peak of human achievement. The mission—Apollo 11—paved the way for decades of space exploration and sparked imagination across generations.

* * *

July 22

Question: On this day in 1795, which treaty ended hostilities between France and Prussia?

Answer: Treaty of Basel

On July 22, 1795, the Treaty of Basel was signed between France and Prussia, ending the War of the First Coalition on that front. The agreement allowed Prussia to withdraw from the anti-French alliance and helped reshape European power dynamics during the Revolution. Basel's terms bolstered France's position and pressured other European powers to adjust their strategies. The treaty's legacy lives in how it reorganized alliances and influenced subsequent negotiations in a long, unsettled era.

* * *

July 23

Question: On this day in 1914, which empire issued the ultimatum to Serbia that helped spark World War I?

Answer: Austria-Hungary

On July 23, 1914, Austria-Hungary presented Serbia with a harsh ultimatum after the assassination of Archduke Franz Ferdinand in Sarajevo. Serbia's reply was seen as insufficient, and Austria-Hungary mobilized, triggering a chain of declarations of war. The ultimatum and ensuing mobilization set off a global conflict that would become World War I. The crisis reshaped borders, empires, and international diplomacy for decades to come.

* * *

July 24

Question: On this day in 1969, which mission's splashdown marked the return of the first crew to land on the Moon?

Answer: Apollo 11

On July 24, 1969, Apollo 11's crew returned to Earth after completing humanity's first crewed Moon landing. The command module Columbia splashed down safely in the Pacific, while the lunar module lingered on the surface. The mission's success fulfilled decades of spaceflight dreams and proved the feasibility of sustained lunar exploration. Its legacy continues to inspire STEM education and international cooperation in exploration.

* * *

July 25

Question: On this day in 1978, who became the first person to be born via in vitro fertilization?

Answer: Louise Brown

On July 25, 1978, Louise Brown was born in Oldham, England—the first baby conceived through in vitro fertilization. Her birth signaled a revolution in reproductive medicine and opened doors for millions of couples struggling with infertility. IVF involved retrieving eggs, fertilizing them outside the body, and transferring embryos back to the uterus. The achievement sparked ongoing ethical, medical, and social conversations about biotechnology, parenthood, and what counts as natural.

* * *

July 26

Question: What milestone connected the United States and Europe via a transatlantic cable on this day in 1956?

Answer: TAT-1

On July 26, 1956, the first transatlantic telephone cable, called TAT-1, went into service. This undersea link carried live voice conversations between North America and Europe for the first time. It used repeaters to boost signals across the ocean and made cross-Atlantic calls practical for businesses and families. The achievement marked a turning point in communications, showing that the digital age would rely on vast, long-distance networks rather than ships and mail. It also set the stage for the modern era of global connectivity that would eventually become fiber-optic and internet-based.

* * *

July 27

Question: Which armistice paused major fighting in Korea on this day in 1953?

Answer: Korean War Armistice

On July 27, 1953, representatives from North Korea, China, and the United Nations Command signed the Korean War

Armistice at Panmunjom. It halted active hostilities and established the Korean Demilitarized Zone that still divides the peninsula. Although it paused fighting, it stopped short of a formal peace treaty, leaving the war technically unresolved. The armistice reshaped regional security and influenced later peace negotiations in Asia.

* * *

JULY 28

Question: Which action by Austria-Hungary began World War I on this day in 1914?

Answer: Austria-Hungary declares war on Serbia

On July 28, 1914, Austria-Hungary declared war on Serbia after a period of escalating tensions and diplomatic ultimatums. Russia began to mobilize, followed by Germany, pulling more nations into the conflict. Within weeks, alliances across Europe would escalate a regional crisis into a world war. The war would redraw borders, topple empires, and reshape political life across the globe for decades.

* * *

JULY 29

Question: On this day in 1958, which U.S. agency was established to coordinate space exploration?

Answer: NASA

On July 29, 1958, the National Aeronautics and Space Act created NASA. It consolidated federal space efforts and integrated the work of existing programs, including the earlier NACA. NASA's mission was to compete in the Space Race and push forward the boundaries of science and exploration. The agency's work would culminate in human spaceflight and dramatic advances that forever changed science, technology, and education.

* * *

July 30

Question: What safety program did President Johnson sign into law on this day in 1965?

Answer: Medicare and Medicaid

On July 30, 1965, President Lyndon B. Johnson signed the Social Security Amendments into law. The package created Medicare for Americans aged 65 and older and Medicaid for low-income individuals and families. The laws expanded healthcare access and defined a broader federal role in financing medical care. The legacy of these programs continues to shape American health policy and debates to this day.

* * *

July 31

Question: On this day in 1914, which nation ordered full mobilization that set the stage for World War I?

Answer: Germany

On July 31, 1914, Germany ordered full mobilization as the July Crisis spiraled toward war. The move leveraged the German general staff's plans for a swift western campaign, while keeping pressure on the eastern front. That decision triggered a domino effect among Europe's great powers, dragging ally commitments into a wider conflict. Within days, a regional crisis had escalated into a continental war that would redraw maps and topple empires. The moment shows how mobilization and alliance politics can push the world from tension to total war.

8

AUGUST

August 1

Question: On this day in 1914, which country declared war on Russia, igniting World War I?

Answer: Germany

On August 1, 1914, Germany declared war on Russia, marking the first major escalation of World War I. Russia's mobilization in response to the crisis over the Balkans triggered a chain reaction among the great powers. Within days, France and Britain were drawn into the conflict, and alliances pulled much of Europe into war. The decision set the stage for a brutal conflict that would reshape international borders and politics for decades. The date is often cited as the moment when a continental crisis turned into a world war.

* * *

August 2

Question: On this day in 1934, which leader merged the offices of president and chancellor to become the Führer of Germany?

Answer: Adolf Hitler

On August 2, 1934, Adolf Hitler merged the offices of president and chancellor, consolidating his grip on the state. With President Hindenburg's death, the move effectively gave him supreme authority over both the government and the military. The fusion formalized the Nazi dictatorship and centralized control over the state, the army, and the party. This consolidation paved the way for aggressive expansion and atrocities committed during the coming years.

* * *

August 3

Question: On this day in 1492, which navigator left the Canary Islands on his first voyage to the New World?

Answer: Christopher Columbus

On August 3, 1492, Christopher Columbus departed from the Canary Islands aboard the Niña, Pinta, and Santa María. Sponsored by the Spanish Crown, his voyage aimed to find a westward route to Asia. Although he never reached the Asian coast, he landed in the Bahamas later that year, marking the first lasting European contact with many Caribbean cultures. His voyage ushered in widespread cross-Atlantic exploration, colonization, and exchange—often called the Columbian Exchange.

* * *

AUGUST 4

Question: On this day in 1789, what decrees abolished feudal privileges in France?

Answer: The August Decrees

On August 4, 1789, the National Assembly issued the August Decrees. These decrees abolished feudal privileges enjoyed by the nobility and clergy, ending dues and tithes tied to the old regime. They proclaimed equality under the law and asserted popular sovereignty over the feudal privileges that had long governed rural life. Though these measures did not solve all economic grievances, they became a catalyst for further revolutionary change.

* * *

AUGUST 5

Question: On this day in 1962, which iconic actress and sex symbol died in Los Angeles?

Answer: Marilyn Monroe

On August 5, 1962, Marilyn Monroe was found dead in her Los Angeles home. Her death shocked fans and sparked endless speculation about her private life and the pressures of stardom. Monroe's performances—'Gentlemen Prefer Blondes', 'Some Like It Hot'—and her public persona helped redefine Hollywood glamour. Her untimely death intensified debates about studio control, mental health, and celebrity culture in mid-20th-century America.

* * *

AUGUST 6

Question: On this day in 1945, which city was the target of the first atomic bomb used in warfare?

Answer: Hiroshima

On August 6, 1945, the United States dropped an atomic bomb on Hiroshima, a city with military significance. The blast killed tens of thousands instantly and unleashed radiation that caused long-term suffering. The destruction stunned the world and forced leaders to confront the dawn of nuclear warfare. Hiroshima's devastation reshaped military strategy, international diplomacy, and public imagination about technology's power. Hiroshima's memory has since become a poignant memorial to peace and the consequences of war.

* * *

AUGUST 7

Question: On this day in 1942, what major Allied operation began in the Solomon Islands?

Answer: Guadalcanal

On August 7, 1942, U.S. Marines and Army troops landed on Guadalcanal, initiating a brutal campaign against Japanese forces. The battle for Guadalcanal dragged on for months, mixing jungle fighting with relentless air and sea combat. It marked the first major Allied offensive against Japan in the Pacific and helped halt Tokyo's southern advance. The campaign strained supply lines, tested new weapons and tactics, and began a shift in momentum in the Pacific War. The island would remain a focal point of Allied strategy through 1942–43.

* * *

AUGUST 8

Question: On this day in 1963, which high-profile British crime involved tampering with a Royal Mail train and stealing cash?

Answer: Great Train Robbery

On August 8, 1963, the Great Train Robbery unfolded on the Royal Mail train at Bridego Bridge in Buckinghamshire. The gang halted the train, bound staff, and escaped with around £2.6 million. The incident captivated the nation, leading to a massive manhunt and arrests in the following years. It also influenced popular culture and inspired many subsequent heist stories and security reforms. The legacy of the robbery endures in UK crime lore.

* * *

AUGUST 9

Question: On this day in 1945, which city became the second to be hit by an atomic bomb in warfare?

Answer: Nagasaki

On August 9, 1945, Nagasaki was devastated by a plutonium-fueled explosion, following Hiroshima earlier in the month. The blast killed tens of thousands instantly and caused lasting injuries from radiation. The event intensified calls for peace and nuclear restraint while accelerating Japan's path toward surrender later that month. Nagasaki's memory has shaped anti-nuclear movements, memorials, and international treaties aimed at preventing such devastation again. The dual bombings dramatically altered how nations think about war and power.

* * *

August 10

Question: On this day in 1792, which royal residence in Paris was stormed, signaling the collapse of the French monarchy?

Answer: Tuileries Palace

On August 10, 1792, crowds stormed the Tuileries Palace, the seat of royal authority in Paris. King Louis XVI and his queen found themselves hunted by revolutionary crowds and soon lost any real political power. The assault precipitated the suspension of the monarchy and set the Revolution on a more radical course. It also forced the royal family into dangerous proximity with the Paris mob, underscoring the fragility of the Ancien Régime. The event remains a symbolic turning point in the French Revolution.

August 11

Question: On this day in 1965, in which Los Angeles neighborhood did civil unrest begin, later associated with a major urban uprising?

Answer: Watts

On August 11, 1965, the Watts neighborhood of Los Angeles erupted in six days of unrest following a controversial police encounter. The violence highlighted racial inequality, policing practices, and economic disparity across American cities. Dozens were killed and hundreds injured as looting and arson spread, drawing in the National Guard. The uprising spurred investigations and policy debates about civil rights, urban poverty, and policing reforms that continued for years. The Watts Riots remain a watershed moment in the Civil Rights era, signaling the urgent need for systemic change.

* * *

August 12

Question: On this day in 1981, what was the name of the personal computer released by a major American company that helped popularize home computing?

Answer: IBM PC

On August 12, 1981, IBM introduced the IBM PC, a personal computer that would reshape offices and homes. Its widely adopted design opened the door for a thriving ecosystem of software and compatible hardware. MS-DOS provided the software backbone that helped the machine spread beyond

IBM's own sales. Within a few years, PC-compatible machines eclipsed the original, launching a revolution in productivity and digital culture.

* * *

AUGUST 13

Question: On this day in 1961, what barrier began to physically separate East and West Berlin?

Answer: Berlin Wall

On August 13, 1961, construction of the Berlin Wall began, physically sealing off the border between East and West Berlin. It was built by the East German government with Soviet support to stem emigration and defections. For nearly three decades families were separated, travel between the sides restricted, and the city divided. Its fall in 1989 became a powerful symbol of the Cold War's end and the reunification of Germany.

* * *

AUGUST 14

Question: On this day in 1947, which new nation celebrated independence from British rule as the subcontinent partitioned into two states?

Answer: Pakistan

On August 14, 1947, Pakistan celebrated independence from British rule as the subcontinent partitioned into two states. Mass migrations and violence followed as Muslims moved to

Pakistan and Hindus and Sikhs moved to India. The Punjab and Bengal regions were partitioned with lines drawn by colonial administrators, creating new boundaries. This moment reshaped South Asian politics and set patterns of regional relations that endure today.

* * *

August 15

Question: On this day in 1947, which country celebrated independence from British rule, launching the world's largest democracy?

Answer: India

On August 15, 1947, India gained independence from British rule, launching the world's largest democracy. The moment followed years of nonviolent resistance led by Gandhi, Nehru, and countless activists. Partition accompanied independence, creating Pakistan to the west and east, and triggering massive migrations. India set out on a challenging path of nation-building, governance, and pluralism that continues to define its story.

* * *

August 16

Question: What musician died on this day in 1977, earning the title 'King of Rock and Roll'?

Answer: Elvis Presley

On August 16th, 1977, Elvis Presley died at Graceland in Memphis. His sudden passing closed a chapter on a performer who fused gospel, blues, and country into a global pop phenomenon. Dubbed the 'King of Rock and Roll,' Elvis's electrifying stage presence helped reshape popular music and performance. His legacy lives on in the generations of artists he inspired and in the enduring popularity of his recordings.

August 17

Question: Which music festival was in full swing on this day in 1969 and became a defining moment of the era?

Answer: Woodstock

On August 17th, 1969, Woodstock—the three-day festival near Bethel, New York—was in full swing. An estimated 400,000 to 500,000 young people gathered to hear legendary acts and soak up a culture of peace, love, and amplified guitars. Although weather and logistics tested the crowd, the event became a defining moment of the era and a lasting symbol of counterculture. Woodstock reshaped how festivals were conceived and remembered, influencing music, fashion, and social movements for decades. Its iconic imagery endures in film, music, and popular memory.

* * *

AUGUST 18

Question: Which amendment granted women the right to vote on this day in 1920?

Answer: Nineteenth Amendment

On August 18th, 1920, the Nineteenth Amendment to the U.S. Constitution was ratified, granting American women the right to vote. It prohibited government denial of suffrage based on sex, following decades of organizing and activism. The Tennessee ratification helped push the amendment over the constitutional threshold. The change dramatically expanded political participation and reshaped elections and public life.

* * *

AUGUST 19

Question: What event began on this day in 1991, when hardliners attempted to oust Soviet leader Mikhail Gorbachev?

Answer: August Coup

On August 19th, 1991, the Soviet leadership announced a state of emergency and detained Mikhail Gorbachev as part of the so-called August Coup. Hardliners hoped to roll back reforms and preserve the old system. Mass protests and political pushback, led by figures like Boris Yeltsin, doomed the coup within days. The failure accelerated the dissolution of the Soviet Union and reshaped Europe's political landscape.

* * *

AUGUST 20

Question: What invasion began on this day in 1968, when Warsaw Pact troops entered Czechoslovakia to crush the Prague Spring?

Answer: Invasion of Czechoslovakia

On August 20th, 1968, Warsaw Pact troops rolled into Czechoslovakia, crushing the Prague Spring reforms. Reformers had sought to loosen censorship and introduce liberalizing changes within a socialist framework. The invasion signaled a hard line from the Soviet Union and the Brezhnev Doctrine, which asserted the right to intervene. Normalisation followed, tightening control and ending the reform era. The event marked a turning point in the Cold War and shaped Eastern Europe's political trajectory for years to come.

* * *

AUGUST 21

Question: On this day in 1831, who led a major slave revolt in Virginia?

Answer: Nat Turner

On August 21, 1831, Nat Turner led a rebellion in Southampton County, Virginia. The uprising killed dozens of white settlers and spread fear through the region. Turner and several of his followers were captured and executed after a few days of violent clashes. The rebellion prompted a harsh crackdown on enslaved people and stricter laws in Virginia and beyond. Historians view it as a pivotal moment that intensified the national debate over slavery, influencing abolitionist sentiment and Southern political responses for years to come.

* * *

August 22

Question: On this day in 1485, which battle secured Henry Tudor's claim and ended the Wars of the Roses?

Answer: Bosworth Field

On August 22, 1485, the Battle of Bosworth Field decided the outcome of the Wars of the Roses. Richard III was killed in combat, and Henry Tudor claimed the throne as Henry VII. The victory established Tudor rule and began a relatively stable period under a centralized monarchy. The battle reshaped English politics and laid groundwork for a new era of governance and expansion. Its legacy echoed through the Tudor dynasty's reforms and the shaping of modern Britain.

* * *

August 23

Question: On this day in 1305, which Scottish leader was captured by English forces following a betrayal near Glasgow?

Answer: William Wallace

On August 23, 1305, William Wallace, the renowned Scottish leader of the resistance against English rule, was captured near Glasgow after a betrayal. He was taken to London, where he faced execution later that year. Wallace's capture dealt a severe blow to the early Scottish struggle for independence, though his legend would inspire future resistance. His story would remain a powerful symbol of Scottish national identity for generations to come.

AUGUST 24

Question: On this day in 410, which city was sacked by the Visigoths, signaling a turning point in the Western Roman Empire?

Answer: Rome

On August 24, 410, Rome was sacked by the Visigoths under King Alaric. The event marked a dramatic shift in the perception of Roman power and signaled the empire's vulnerability. The sack disrupted daily life and trade, reverberating across the Mediterranean world. Historians view it as a watershed moment that contributed to the long-term decline of Western Roman authority and catalyzed religious and political changes in Europe.

* * *

AUGUST 25

Question: On this day in 1944, which city was liberated by Allied forces, signaling a turning point in Western Europe during World War II?

Answer: Paris

On August 25, 1944, Paris rose in celebration as Allied and Free French forces liberated the city from Nazi occupation. The freeing of the city became a potent symbol of resistance and the turning tide in Western Europe. Parisians took to the streets in massive celebrations as the city rejoined the Free World. The liberation boosted Allied morale and helped pave the way for the subsequent liberation of nearby territories and countries.

* * *

AUGUST 26

Question: On this day in 1920, which constitutional amendment was certified granting women the right to vote?

Answer: Nineteenth Amendment

On August 26, 1920, the United States certified the Nineteenth Amendment, cementing women's suffrage. It granted women the legal right to vote in federal and state elections. The long, hard-fought campaign by suffragists and allies across decades made this possible. Its adoption reshaped American democracy and opened doors for women in public life. Its legacy continues to echo in ongoing fights for voting rights and representation.

* * *

AUGUST 27

Question: On this day in 1883, which volcanic island produced one of the most violent eruptions in recorded history?

Answer: Krakatoa

On August 27, 1883, Krakatoa erupted with cataclysmic force, tearing apart the volcanic island in the Sunda Strait. The explosions hurled ash clouds into the atmosphere, triggered tsunamis, and colored sunsets around the world for years. People as far away as Australia and Africa heard the blasts. The eruption reshaped the geography of the Krakatoa archipelago and left a lasting mark on geologic science. Its dramatic event helped spur early volcanology and inspired generations of researchers.

* * *

AUGUST 28

Question: On this day in 1963, which leader delivered the I Have a Dream speech during the March on Washington?

Answer: Martin Luther King Jr.

On August 28, 1963, Martin Luther King Jr. delivered the I Have a Dream speech on the National Mall, during a watershed moment of the American Civil Rights Movement. His call for equality and nonviolence helped galvanize support for landmark civil rights legislation. The march drew hundreds of thousands to Washington, D.C., and became a defining moment in 20th-century social justice. King's rhetoric resonated beyond the United States, fueling other movements for freedom around the world. The speech remains a touchstone of American rhetoric and advocacy.

* * *

AUGUST **29**

Question: On this day in 1949, which country detonated its first atomic bomb?

Answer: Soviet Union

On August 29, 1949, the Soviet Union detonated its first atomic bomb, code-named First Lightning. The test ended the United States' monopoly on nuclear weapons and sparked a robust arms race of the Cold War era. Scientists and policymakers debated the ethics, deterrence, and geopolitical implications of nuclear weapons. The blast reverberated through international relations, influencing treaties, alliances, and defense strategies for decades. Its legacy continues to shape debates about security and power in the modern world.

* * *

AUGUST **30**

Question: On this day in 1914, which battle on the Eastern Front concluded with a German victory over Russia?

Answer: Battle of Tannenberg

On August 30, 1914, the Battle of Tannenberg on the Eastern Front ended with a decisive German victory over Russia. German generals Paul von Hindenburg and Erich Ludendorff encircled and destroyed the Russian Second Army. The victory halted Russian offensives and changed the early momentum of World War I. The triumph boosted German morale and established Hindenburg's and Ludendorff's reputations. Its consequences shaped Eastern Front warfare and set the tone for a harsh winter campaign.

* * *

AUGUST 31

Question: Who died on this day in 1997, causing worldwide mourning and an outpouring of tributes?

Answer: Diana, Princess of Wales

On August 31, 1997, Diana, Princess of Wales, died in a car crash in Paris. The crash occurred in the Pont de l'Alma tunnel after a high-speed chase with paparazzi, and her companion Dodi Fayed and their driver Henri Paul also died. Her death provoked a wave of global mourning and intensified debates about media intrusion and royal life in the modern era. In Britain, millions watched the funeral, and the outpouring of tributes solidified Diana's image as the 'People's Princess' while shifting philanthropic focus within the royal family. Her legacy continues to shape discussions about privacy, charity, and the responsibilities of public figures.

9

SEPTEMBER

September 1

Question: On this day in 1939, which invasion marked the start of World War II?

Answer: Invasion of Poland

On September 1, 1939, Germany invaded Poland, launching World War II. Blitzkrieg tactics relied on rapid air and ground assaults that overwhelmed Polish defenses. Britain and France declared war on Germany within days, pulling much of Europe into the conflict. The invasion redrew the map of Europe and set a course for a war that would shape the rest of the century.

* * *

SEPTEMBER 2

Question: On this day in 1666, which city suffered a devastating fire that swept through its medieval center?

Answer: London

On September 2, 1666, the Great Fire of London began in a bakery on Pudding Lane. Over four days, wooden houses and narrow streets fanned the flames across the city. St. Paul's Cathedral and thousands of homes fell to the blaze, changing the skyline forever. The fire prompted a massive rebuilding effort led by Sir Christopher Wren, reshaping London's future.

* * *

SEPTEMBER 3

Question: On this day in 1939, which two nations declared war on Germany, signaling their entry into World War II?

Answer: Britain and France

On September 3, 1939, Britain and France declared war after Germany's invasion of Poland. The move ended years of appeasement debates and launched the Phoney War period. Military mobilization and war planning swept across Europe as nations prepared for a long conflict. The declarations transformed the political landscape and set the stage for a truly global war.

* * *

SEPTEMBER 4

Question: On this day in 1957, which city became the flashpoint of desegregation as federal troops escorted nine Black students into a high school?

Answer: Little Rock

On September 4, 1957, federal troops were sent to Little Rock, Arkansas, to enforce the desegregation of Central High School. The Arkansas National Guard had been blocking the nine Black students, creating a tense national showdown. President Eisenhower federalized the Guard and ordered troops to protect the students as they attended classes. The Little Rock Crisis became a watershed moment in the Civil Rights Movement, proving federal authority could enforce school integration.

* * *

SEPTEMBER 5

Question: On this day in 1977, which spacecraft was launched to explore the outer planets?

Answer: Voyager 1

On September 5, 1977, NASA launched Voyager 1 as part of a grand planetary tour. Its sister ship, Voyager 2, followed along a different trajectory to visit Jupiter, Saturn, and beyond. Flying past Jupiter in 1979 and Saturn in 1980, Voyager 1 captured iconic images that reshaped our sense of the solar system. Today, Voyager 1 continues to drift through interstellar space, carrying a golden record of Earth's sounds and stories.

SEPTEMBER 6

Question: Who shot President William McKinley on this day in 1901?

Answer: Leon Czolgosz

On September 6, 1901, President William McKinley was shot by anarchist Leon Czolgosz during a public reception at the Pan-American Exposition in Buffalo. Although he initially survived, he died on September 14 after complications from the wounds. McKinley's assassination prompted a sweeping expansion of presidential protection and helped legitimize the Secret Service's role guarding the president. The event cast long shadows over American politics, influencing security protocols for decades to come.

SEPTEMBER 7

Question: Which country declared independence from Portugal on this day in 1822?

Answer: Brazil

On September 7, 1822, Brazil declared independence from Portugal. Prince Dom Pedro I, who had ruled in Brazil as part of the colonial framework, took the bold step that ended centuries of colonial ties. The new nation became the Empire of Brazil with Pedro I as its first Emperor. Independence reshaped South American politics and inspired other colonies to pursue autonomy.

* * *

September 8

Question: What TV series premiered on this day in 1966, introducing Captain Kirk?

Answer: Star Trek

On September 8, 1966, Star Trek debuted on NBC with the pilot 'The Man Trap.' The crew of the Starship Enterprise sparked a cultural phenomenon that reshaped science fiction and mainstream imagination. The show introduced a diverse, mission-driven team exploring ethical questions through space travel. Its enduring legacy continues in films, spin-offs, and a devoted fandom.

* * *

September 9

Question: Which iconic musician made his first national television appearance on The Ed Sullivan Show on this day in 1956?

Answer: Elvis Presley

On September 9, 1956, Elvis delivered a performance that would define rock 'n' roll for a generation. The appearance drew mass attention, generating controversy over his provocative dancing and launching his meteoric rise to fame. The broadcast helped propel his career and cemented the Ed Sullivan Show as a national stage for modern pop. Elvis's breakthrough era signaled a sea change in American popular culture.

* * *

SEPTEMBER 10

Question: What scientific facility began first beam operations on this day in 2008?

Answer: Large Hadron Collider

On September 10, 2008, the Large Hadron Collider at CERN began circulating its first proton beams. This milestone marked the start of a new generation of particle-physics experiments aiming to probe the Higgs field and fundamental forces. Engineers and scientists spent decades building the 27-kilometer ring and the thousands of magnets that guide particles around it. Although the collider would not immediately uncover dramatic new physics, it opened a window to a universe of tiny, powerful mysteries.

* * *

SEPTEMBER 11

Question: On this day in 2001, which major New York City landmark was struck by a hijacked plane?

Answer: World Trade Center

On September 11th, 2001, four hijacked planes launched a sequence of attacks across the United States. The most iconic images came from the World Trade Center in New York City, where both towers were struck and ultimately fell. The attacks precipitated sweeping changes in international security, U.S. foreign policy, and global anti-terrorism efforts. Memorials, resilience, and the stories of first responders and survivors continue to shape collective memory of the day. It remains a watershed moment in modern history, reshaping how nations think about safety and threat.

* * *

SEPTEMBER 12

Question: On this day in 1814, which fort in Baltimore Harbor withstood a British bombardment that inspired a famous national anthem?

Answer: Fort McHenry

On September 12th, 1814, American forces defended Fort McHenry during a night of bombardment. The fort's steadfast defense against the British fleet kept the flag flying above Baltimore and inspired Francis Scott Key to write a poem that would become The Star-Spangled Banner. The episode energized American morale during the War of 1812 and became a lasting symbol of resilience. Fort McHenry's endurance helped cement a sense of national identity at a crucial moment in U.S. history. The story endures in music, memory, and the ongoing celebration of American endurance.

* * *

SEPTEMBER 13

Question: On this day in 1759, which city in Canada was captured by British forces during the Seven Years' War?

Answer: Quebec

On September 13th, 1759, British troops under General James Wolfe defeated the French on the Plains of Abraham and captured Quebec. This victory shifted the balance of power in North America toward Britain, setting the stage for British dominance in Canada. The fall of Quebec helped precipitate the end of French colonial ambitions in much of North America. The capture also influenced subsequent treaties and borders that shaped North American geopolitics for generations. Quebec's fall became a defining moment in the colonial struggle between Britain and France.

* * *

SEPTEMBER 14

Question: On this day in 1901, which U.S. president died after being shot?

Answer: William McKinley

On September 14th, 1901, President William McKinley died due to complications from an assassination attempt earlier that month. His death accelerated Theodore Roosevelt's ascent to the presidency and reshaped American leadership at the dawn of the 20th century. The event intensified debates over presidential security and succession at a time of rapid industrial growth and reform movements. McKinley's presidency had overseen economic expansion, imperial expansion, and complex domestic policy, and his passing marked a pivotal transition in American politics. Roosevelt's energetic approach would define the era that followed.

* * *

SEPTEMBER 15

Question: On this day in 1940, which air campaign saw a massive bombing of London that became a symbol of Britain's resilience?

Answer: The Blitz

On September 15th, 1940, the Luftwaffe intensified air raids on Britain, with London bearing the brunt of the assault. This period is widely remembered as the Blitz, a brutal chapter of World War II that tested civilian endurance and national morale. The sustained bombing extended to many British cities and prompted widespread civil defense measures. Britain's ability to endure and continue the war effort helped sustain Allied strategy and ultimately contributed to the campaign's turn in favor of the Allies. The Blitz reshaped civilian life and became a defining symbol of resilience in wartime Europe.

* * *

SEPTEMBER 16

Question: On this day in 1620, which ship departed Plymouth, England, bound for the New World?

Answer: Mayflower

On September 16, 1620, the Mayflower departed Plymouth, England, carrying 102 passengers and crew bound for the Virginia Colony. A fierce Atlantic crossing tested their resolve as storms and uncertain winds pushed them off course. They eventually anchored at Cape Cod in present-day Massachusetts, where settlers would establish Plymouth Colony. The voyage is remembered as a foundational moment in early American colonization and the story of religious migration.

* * *

SEPTEMBER 17

Question: On this day in 1787, which document was signed by delegates at the Constitutional Convention?

Answer: U.S. Constitution

On September 17, 1787, the delegates at the Constitutional Convention signed the U.S. Constitution. The document created a new framework of government that balanced power between the federal and state authorities. It replaced the weaker Articles of Confederation after debates over representation, veto power, and the scope of federal authority. Over the centuries, the Constitution has guided American politics and inspired reform movements around the world.

* * *

SEPTEMBER 18

Question: On this day in 1851, which newspaper published its first edition?

Answer: The New York Times

On September 18, 1851, The New-York Daily Times published its first edition. The paper was founded by Henry Jarvis Raymond and George Jones and aimed at providing straightforward reporting. It would grow into a national daily with a reputation for reliability and in-depth coverage. Today The New York Times is one of the most influential news outlets in the world.

* * *

SEPTEMBER 19

Question: On this day in 1796, which president delivered his Farewell Address to the nation?

Answer: George Washington

On September 19, 1796, George Washington delivered his Farewell Address to the nation. In it, he warned about entangling alliances and the dangers of faction in American politics. He urged the young republic to prioritize virtue, the Constitution, and a balanced federal system. The speech helped set norms for peaceful transfer of power and remains a touchstone for democratic practice.

* * *

SEPTEMBER 20

Question: On this day in 1519, which explorer's fleet departed Seville, beginning the first circumnavigation of the globe?

Answer: Ferdinand Magellan

On September 20, 1519, Ferdinand Magellan's fleet departed Seville, beginning the first circumnavigation of the globe. The voyage proved that the Earth is round and that oceans connect continents in a global trading network, though Magellan himself did not survive the journey. Only one of the five ships completed the voyage, the Victoria, under the command of Juan Sebastián Elcano. The expedition opened new sea routes and reshaped global politics and trade.

* * *

September 21

Question: On this day in 1862, which president issued the Preliminary Emancipation Proclamation that redefined the war's aims and began freeing enslaved people in Confederate-held territories?

Answer: Abraham Lincoln

On September 22, 1862, President Abraham Lincoln announced the Preliminary Emancipation Proclamation. The move reframed the Civil War as a fight against slavery and allowed for the enlistment of Black soldiers in the Union Army. It proclaimed that enslaved people in rebelling states would be free as of January 1, 1863, if those states did not return to the Union. The proclamation did not immediately free enslaved people in border states or those under Union control, but it fundamentally changed the war's moral and political calculus. Its publication paved the way for the eventual abolition of slavery in the United States with the 13th Amendment.

* * *

SEPTEMBER 22

Question: On this day in 1846, which planet was officially discovered thanks to predictions by Urbain Le Verrier and observed by Johann Galle?

Answer: Neptune

On September 23, 1846, Neptune was discovered after mathematical predictions by Le Verrier and independent work by Adams. The first good observations came from Johann Galle at the Berlin Observatory, confirming the planet's presence beyond Uranus. The discovery world-shaken both astronomy and science because it was the first planet located by mathematical prediction rather than direct observation. Neptune's recognition expanded our understanding of the solar system and orbiting bodies. The event also showcased the power of collaborative science and predictive mathematics.

* * *

SEPTEMBER 23

Question: On this day in 1789, which act established the three-tier federal judiciary of the United States, creating district and circuit courts and setting up the Supreme Court?

Answer: Judiciary Act

On September 24, 1789, the Judiciary Act established the structure of the federal judiciary. It created the district courts and circuit courts and defined the jurisdiction and powers of federal judges. The act also helped set the number of Supreme Court justices and laid groundwork for critical judicial procedures still in use. This was a pivotal step in turning the new Constitution into an operable framework for law and governance. Its legacy includes the enduring balance of power between the federal courts and the other branches.

* * *

SEPTEMBER 24

Question: On this day in 1513, which explorer is traditionally credited with reaching la Florida, a voyage that would leave a lasting mark on European and Native American history?

Answer: Ponce de León

On September 25, 1513, the Spanish explorer Juan Ponce de León is associated with landing in Florida and naming the land La Florida. His voyage, sponsored by the Crown, aimed to find new lands and the fabled Fountain of Youth in tales that swirled around his expedition. While the exact details and dates are debated among historians, this moment became a defining part of early European exploration of North America. The Florida landing opened ongoing Spanish interaction with the Southeast and set the stage for later colonial dynamics. The myth of youth and renewal surrounding de León's voyage endures in cultural memory.

* * *

SEPTEMBER 25

Question: On this day in 1789, which foundational legal framework for the U.S. judiciary came into effect, shaping courts across the new nation?

Answer: Judiciary Act

On September 24, 1789, the Judiciary Act established the federal judiciary as a functional branch of government. It created district courts, circuit courts, and defined the role and jurisdiction of federal judges and justices. The act also formalized the relationship between state and federal courts, helping to unify legal processes under the Constitution. Its enduring legacy is the modern structure of the U.S. court system, including the Supreme Court and lower federal courts. This day marks a cornerstone in American legal history.

* * *

SEPTEMBER 26

Question: On this day in 1960, what event marked the first televised presidential debate between John F. Kennedy and Richard Nixon?

Answer: First televised JFK-Nixon debate

On September 26, 1960, the first televised presidential debate between John F. Kennedy and Richard Nixon took place. It established a new standard for political campaigning, with voters judging candidates by appearance as well as by words. Nixon's reserve and Kennedy's telegenic charisma contrasted in the minds of viewers. The broadcast underscored television's power in shaping political careers and public perception.

* * *

SEPTEMBER 27

Question: On this day in 1821, which country achieved independence from Spain as Iturbide's forces entered its capital?

Answer: Mexico

On September 27, 1821, Mexican independence was secured as Iturbide's Army of the Three Guarantees entered Mexico City. Earlier that year, the Plan of Iguala had laid out independence and a constitutional framework for the emerging nation. The news transformed a colony into an independent nation and reshaped the map of the Americas. It set Mexico on a course toward constitutionalism and nationhood in the 19th century.

* * *

SEPTEMBER 28

Question: On this day in 1928, what antibiotic did Alexander Fleming discover when a mold contaminated a Petri dish inhibited bacterial growth?

Answer: Penicillin

On September 28, 1928, Fleming observed that a mold-contaminated Staphylococcus plate prevented nearby bacteria from growing. That observation led to the discovery of penicillin, the first true antibiotic. Its development, aided by Florey and Chain, launched the era of antimicrobial medicine. Penicillin's success revolutionized medicine, turning once-lethal infections into treatable conditions.

* * *

SEPTEMBER 29

Question: On this day in 1996, what gaming console did Nintendo release in North America, introducing 3D gameplay?

Answer: Nintendo 64

On September 29, 1996, Nintendo released the Nintendo 64 in North America, signaling a shift toward real-time 3D graphics. Its launch title, Super Mario 64, demonstrated immersive 3D gameplay and set new industry benchmarks. The cartridge-based design delivered snappier load times and helped define early 3D hardware standards. The release catalyzed a generation of iconic games and reshaped the console market.

* * *

SEPTEMBER 30

Question: On this day in 1938, what accord did Britain, France, Germany, and Italy sign to appease Hitler over Czechoslovakia?

Answer: Munich Agreement

On September 30, 1938, the Munich Agreement was signed by Britain, France, Germany, and Italy to appease Hitler over Czechoslovakia. The pact epitomized the era's policy of appeasement, trading concessions for the illusion of peace. Hitler's subsequent actions proved that appeasement only postponed inevitable conflict. The agreement's legacy is a stark reminder of how diplomacy and power can intersect with dangerous consequences.

OCTOBER

October 1

Question: On this day in 1908, which car model began mass production at Ford's Highland Park plant?

Answer: Model T

On October 1st, 1908, Ford's Model T began production at the Highland Park plant, thanks to Henry Ford's moving assembly line. The car was designed to be affordable and easy to repair, using standardized parts. Its mass production revolutionized manufacturing, making personal mobility accessible to millions. The Model T's success reshaped American life, cities, and industry, and its legacy dominates car design to this day.

* * *

October 2

Question: On this day in 1835, which battle began the Texas Revolution?

Answer: Battle of Gonzales

On October 2, 1835, Texans faced Mexican troops at Gonzales, sparking the Texas Revolution. The famous 'Come and take it' cannon became a symbol of Texan defiance. The clash led to a wider conflict that eventually secured Texas independence. Gonzales set the tone for a struggle that would include sieges and battles at the Alamo and San Jacinto.

* * *

October 3

Question: On this day in 1995, which famous NFL star was acquitted of murder charges?

Answer: O. J. Simpson

On October 3, 1995, the jury found O. J. Simpson not guilty of the murders of Nicole Brown Simpson and Ron Goldman. The trial became a cultural touchstone, stirring debates about race, celebrity, and media influence. The verdict did not end the public conversation—if anything, it amplified it. Simpson's case left a lasting mark on how celebrity trials are covered and perceived.

* * *

OCTOBER 4

Question: On this day in 1957, what was the first artificial satellite launched into orbit?

Answer: Sputnik

On October 4, 1957, the Soviet Union launched Sputnik 1, the first artificial satellite. Its beeping radio signals announced that space was no longer a distant dream, but a real frontier. Sputnik kicked off the space race and spurred an era of rapid scientific and technological innovation. Its legacy persists in satellite communications, GPS, weather monitoring, and deep-space exploration.

* * *

OCTOBER 5

Question: On this day in 1994, which international day designated to honor teachers worldwide is observed?

Answer: World Teachers' Day

On October 5, 1994, UNESCO designated World Teachers' Day to celebrate the teaching profession. The designation honored teachers' essential role in building educated, informed societies. The day highlights ongoing needs— teacher training, fair pay, and classroom conditions. Every year since, communities around the globe mark the date with gratitude and renewed commitment to education.

* * *

OCTOBER 6

Question: On this day in 1973, which two countries launched a surprise attack on Israel to begin the Yom Kippur War?

Answer: Egypt and Syria

On October 6, 1973, Egypt and Syria launched a surprise attack on Israel, igniting the Yom Kippur War. The coordinated assault caught Israel off guard on a holy day and escalated regional tensions into a full-scale conflict. The fighting drew in Cold War powers, with the United States and the Soviet Union backing their respective allies. A fragile ceasefire followed later in October, but the war forever altered Middle East diplomacy and helped set the stage for later peace negotiations, including Egypt–Israel accords. The human cost was high, and the war reshaped military planning and intelligence thinking for decades.

* * *

OCTOBER 7

Question: On this day in 1571, which major naval battle took place between the Holy League and the Ottoman Empire?

Answer: Battle of Lepanto

On October 7, 1571, off the coast of Greece, the Holy League's fleet defeated the Ottoman navy at the Battle of Lepanto. The Christian coalition, led by Don John of Austria, united Venetian and other Mediterranean powers against the Ottomans. The victory checked Ottoman naval supremacy in the Mediterranean for decades. It became a symbolic turning point in Christian Europe and a landmark in naval warfare history. The battle's legacy lived on in art, literature, and the broader contest between empires.

* * *

OCTOBER 8

Question: On this day in 1871, which city suffered a devastating fire that destroyed much of its downtown?

Answer: Chicago

On October 8, 1871, the Great Chicago Fire swept through the city, fueled by wooden buildings and dry conditions. The flames burned for two days, leaving tens of thousands homeless and reducing much of the downtown to ashes. The disaster spurred sweeping rebuilding codes and the rapid growth of Chicago as a hub of innovation. The city rebuilt with a bold architectural vision, giving rise to skylines and techniques that defined modern urban planning. The Chicago Fire remains a defining moment in the city's history and in 19th-century American urban development.

* * *

OCTOBER 9

Question: On this day in 1962, which country gained independence from Britain?

Answer: Uganda

On October 9, 1962, Uganda achieved independence from Britain, joining the Commonwealth. Milton Obote became prime minister, while Edward Mutesa II served as ceremonial president and monarch. The new nation drafted constitutional arrangements that would soon give way to republican rule amid political tensions. Uganda's independence marked a turning point in East Africa's postcolonial era, influencing neighboring countries as they navigated nation-building, governance, and regional politics. The era that followed featured both optimism and turbulence as new leaders defined national identity.

* * *

OCTOBER 10

Question: On this day in 732, which battle halted Islamic expansion into Western Europe?

Answer: Battle of Tours

On October 10, 732, Charles Martel's Frankish forces defeated the Umayyad army at Tours. The victory is widely remembered as a turning point that halted northern expansion of the Umayyad Caliphate into Western Europe. It helped consolidate Frankish power in Gaul and shaped the religious and political map of medieval Europe. Historians debate the full strategic impact, but the clash has endured as a powerful symbol in European historical memory. The battle's legacy influenced subsequent Christian and European political narratives for centuries.

* * *

OCTOBER 11

Question: On this day in 1968, which mission launched from Cape Kennedy and carried the first crewed Apollo flight after the Apollo 1 tragedy?

Answer: Apollo 7

On October 11, 1968, Apollo 7 blasted off from Cape Kennedy, beginning NASA's first crewed Apollo mission after the fatal Apollo 1 fire. Commanded by Wally Schirra, with Donn F. Eisele and Walter Cunningham aboard, the mission orbited Earth for 11 days. The crew tested life-support systems, spacecraft performance, and endurance in space, proving the command module ready for lunar-era work. The successful flight repaired NASA's confidence and paved the way for Apollo 8's lunar orbit mission. The mission's modest but critical success helped restore public trust in the Apollo program.

* * *

OCTOBER 12

Question: On this day in 1492, which explorer landed in the Bahamas and opened sustained European contact with the Americas?

Answer: Christopher Columbus

On October 12, 1492, Columbus's expedition landed in the Bahamas, marking the first contact between Europe and the Americas in the late 15th century. He and his crew believed they had reached islands off Asia; the reality was a previously unknown continental landmass. News of the voyage spread across Europe, catalyzing sustained transatlantic exploration and colonization. The encounter also carried profound and often devastating consequences for Indigenous peoples. The voyage reshaped global trade, ecosystems, and cultures in ways that still echo today.

* * *

OCTOBER 13

Question: On this day in 1307, which organization was ordered arrested by King Philip IV of France, sparking a crackdown across medieval Europe?

Answer: Knights Templar

On October 13, 1307, King Philip IV of France ordered the arrest of the Knights Templar, initiating a crackdown that echoed across medieval Europe. Facing charges of heresy and other alleged transgressions, many Templar knights were imprisoned and later executed. The purge benefited the French crown and shifted power dynamics in Europe for decades. The order was formally dissolved in the following years, but its legend persists in popular culture. The episode reflects the volatile politics of medieval monarchy, finance, and religious authority.

* * *

OCTOBER 14

Question: On this day in 1066, which battle began the Norman conquest of England?

Answer: Battle of Hastings

On October 14, 1066, the Battle of Hastings concluded with William the Conqueror's forces defeating Harold II and securing Norman rule over England. The victory forged a new ruling dynasty and reshaped the English language, law, and aristocracy. The conquest sparked centuries of cultural exchange and conflict that influenced architecture, governance, and the question of identity in Britain. The event is often treated as a turning point in medieval history. Its legacy endures in the famous Bayeux Tapestry and in countless references to Norman influence.

October 15

Question: On this day in 1582, which reform realigned the calendar by skipping ten days in October?

Answer: Gregorian calendar

On October 15, 1582, Catholic Europe began using the Gregorian calendar to correct drift in the solar year, skipping 10 days in October as the reform took effect in those lands. The change aligned calendar dates with the solar year and the equinox, improving seasonal accuracy for religious and agricultural events. Countries adopting the reform in quick succession created a patchwork of calendars around the world for centuries. The adjustment legacy is visible in how we coordinate time today; not all regions adopted it at once, with some persisting on the Julian calendar for many years. It set the stage for modern international timekeeping and scheduling.

* * *

OCTOBER 16

Question: Who was executed by guillotine on this day in 1793 during the French Revolution?

Answer: Marie Antoinette

On October 16, 1793, Marie Antoinette was executed by guillotine after a swift trial. Her death marked a brutal turning point in the French Revolution and the fall of the Ancien Régime. The queen's life had long symbolized royal privilege to some and political peril to others. The event sent ripples beyond France, affecting European politics and the way revolutions were perceived in the 18th century.

* * *

OCTOBER 17

Question: What major earthquake struck the San Francisco Bay Area on this day in 1989, just before a World Series game?

Answer: Loma Prieta earthquake

On October 17, 1989, the Loma Prieta earthquake struck the San Francisco Bay Area with a magnitude of 6.9. It occurred during Game 3 of the World Series, toppling freeways and igniting fires. The quake shattered assumptions about urban resilience and led to new construction codes and retrofit programs. The event remains a defining moment in California history and a case study in disaster preparedness.

* * *

OCTOBER 18

Question: What territory was formally transferred to the United States on this day in 1867, completing the Alaska Purchase?

Answer: Alaska

On October 18, 1867, the formal transfer ceremony completed the Alaska Purchase, with the United States taking possession of Alaska. The $7.2 million purchase, negotiated by Secretary of State William H. Seward, was controversial at the time. Alaska's vast resources and strategic location would reshape American expansion and foreign policy in the decades that followed. The ceremony symbolized a turning point in 19th-century imperial ambitions.

* * *

OCTOBER 19

Question: What event on this day in 1987 earned the nickname Black Monday?

Answer: Black Monday

On October 19, 1987, stock markets around the world collapsed in what would become known as Black Monday. The Dow Jones Industrial Average fell about 22.6%, marking the largest one-day percentage drop in U.S. history. Rapid program trading and investor panic amplified the decline across global markets. Regulators later introduced circuit breakers to slow down future crashes.

* * *

OCTOBER 20

Question: What land deal was ratified by the United States Senate on this day in 1803, expanding U.S. territory?

Answer: Louisiana Purchase

On October 20, 1803, the United States Senate ratified the Louisiana Purchase. This vote, negotiated by President Thomas Jefferson, doubled the nation's size and opened vast lands for exploration and settlement. The acquisition reshaped U.S. diplomacy and relations with France, fueling westward expansion. It laid the groundwork for the era of Manifest Destiny that would shape American politics for decades.

* * *

OCTOBER 21

Question: On this day in 1805, which British admiral won the Battle of Trafalgar?

Answer: Horatio Nelson

On October 21, 1805, the British fleet under Admiral Horatio Nelson defeated the combined French and Spanish fleets at Trafalgar. Nelson's audacious tactic—breaking the line—broke the enemy center and secured a decisive victory, though he was fatally wounded aboard HMS Victory. The win gave Britain uncontested command of the seas and blunted Napoleon's plans to invade Britain. Nelson's name became a byword for daring leadership and shipboard heroics. The battle reshaped naval power for generations and helped preserve British global dominance through the Napoleonic era.

* * *

OCTOBER 22

Question: On this day in 1962, what measure did President Kennedy announce to prevent Soviet missiles from reaching Cuba?

Answer: Naval quarantine

On October 22, 1962, President John F. Kennedy announced that the United States would impose a naval quarantine around Cuba to prevent the delivery of Soviet missiles. The quarantine differed from a blockade in its legal framing and aimed to avoid an outright act of war. Tensions mounted as Soviet ships approached the quarantine line, placing the world on the brink of nuclear conflict. Behind the scenes, intense diplomacy and back-channel talks eventually led to the missiles' removal. The crisis is remembered as a tense but pivotal moment when careful leadership helped avert catastrophe.

* * *

OCTOBER 23

Question: On this day in 1942, which major North Africa battle began?

Answer: Second Battle of El Alamein

On October 23, 1942, Allied forces under General Bernard Montgomery launched the Second Battle of El Alamein against Axis commander Erwin Rommel. The battle marked a turning point in the Western Desert Campaign, as the Allies gained momentum and began to break Axis supply lines. The victory boosted Allied morale and forced Rommel to retreat into Libya. The campaign's success also secured the Suez Canal, a vital strategic chokepoint for Allied shipping. It is widely considered one of the decisive engagements of the war in North Africa.

* * *

OCTOBER 24

Question: On this day in 1945, which international organization officially came into force?

Answer: United Nations

On October 24, 1945, the United Nations Charter came into effect, inaugurating the United Nations as a global forum for cooperation. The UN emerged from the ashes of World War II as a successor to the League of Nations, with a structure designed to prevent future conflicts. It established core bodies such as the Security Council and General Assembly, and set out principles for peacekeeping, development, and human rights. The organization has since played a central role in diplomacy, humanitarian aid, and international law.

October 24 is United Nations Day to recognize that mission.

* * *

OCTOBER 25

Question: On this day in 1415, which king led English forces at the Battle of Agincourt?

Answer: Henry V

On October 25, 1415, English forces under King Henry V defeated a numerically superior French army at Agincourt. The victory was powered by longbowmen whose arrows pierced French knights and broke their formations. The triumph elevated Henry V's reputation and infused English morale with a storied medieval victory. The battle also highlighted shifts in military technology and leadership that would echo through the Hundred Years' War. Agincourt remains a lasting symbol of courage, strategy, and the uncertainties of medieval combat.

* * *

OCTOBER 26

Question: On this day in 1825, which major waterway opened, reshaping commerce in New York and the United States?

Answer: Erie Canal

On October 26, 1825, the Erie Canal opened to traffic. It linked the Hudson River at Albany with Lake Erie at Buffalo, creating a water route to the Great Lakes. Transport costs plummeted and goods could move from west to east more quickly. Cities along the canal region boomed, and New York City rose as a commercial hub. The canal's success spurred further infrastructure projects and reshaped the nation's economy.

* * *

OCTOBER 27

Question: On this day in 1904, which massive urban transit project opened in New York City?

Answer: New York City Subway

On October 27, 1904, the first section of the New York City Subway opened to the public. The initial line, operated by the Interborough Rapid Transit Company, ran from City Hall to 145th Street in Harlem. It transformed urban life, slashing travel times and enabling neighborhoods to grow. The subway became a symbol of modern urban engineering and a blueprint for cities around the world. Its construction also sparked debates about labor, safety, and funding that shaped transit policy for decades.

* * *

OCTOBER 28

Question: On this day in 1962, which crisis ended with the removal of Soviet missiles from Cuba?

Answer: Cuban Missile Crisis

On October 28, 1962, the Cuban Missile Crisis moved toward resolution as leaders negotiated a settlement. Khrushchev agreed to withdraw Soviet missiles from Cuba in exchange for a U.S. pledge not to invade and a secret deal to remove U.S. missiles from Turkey. The crisis brought the world to the brink of nuclear war and catalyzed a shift toward arms control. A naval quarantine, Kennedy's televised address, and back-channel diplomacy all played critical roles. The resolution left a lasting imprint on Cold War diplomacy and the importance of crisis management.

* * *

OCTOBER 29

Question: On this day in 1929, which infamous stock market crash marked the beginning of the Great Depression?

Answer: Black Tuesday

On October 29, 1929, the stock market collapsed after days of heavy selling. Investors panicked; banks failed; millions of people saw their fortunes wiped out. The crash revealed deep vulnerabilities in the U.S. economy and helped trigger the Great Depression. New policies and regulatory measures would eventually reshape financial policy. Black Tuesday remains a symbol of the fragility of prosperity and the importance of financial safeguards.

* * *

OCTOBER 30

Question: On this day in 1938, which radio broadcast caused mass panic among listeners?

Answer: War of the Worlds

On October 30, 1938, Orson Welles's radio adaptation of The War of the Worlds aired on CBS. Presented as live news bulletins, it sparked panic among some listeners who believed an actual invasion was underway. The incident highlighted the power of broadcast media and the thin line between fiction and reality. In its wake, broadcasters and regulators debated disclaimers, pacing, and the responsibilities of live performance. The War of the Worlds broadcast remains a defining case study in media literacy.

* * *

OCTOBER 31

Question: On this day in 1971, astronauts drove a vehicle on the Moon for the very first time. What was the name of this mission?

Answer: Apollo 15

On July 31, 1971, Apollo 15 astronauts David Scott and James Irwin became the first humans to drive on the lunar surface. Taking the Lunar Roving Vehicle (LRV) for its inaugural spin, they drastically expanded the range of space exploration. The foldable, battery-powered buggy allowed the astronauts to travel much further from their Lunar Module than previous walking missions, ultimately covering over 17 miles (27 km) during their three-day stay. This technological leap transformed our ability to gather geological samples, proving that humanity could not only reach another world, but actually take a road trip on it.

NOVEMBER

November 1

Question: On this day in 1512, which Renaissance artist unveiled the ceiling frescoes of the Sistine Chapel after years of work for the pope?

Answer: Michelangelo

On November 1st, 1512, Michelangelo's Sistine Chapel ceiling was first shown to the public in Vatican City. Painted largely while working high on scaffolding, it turned a grueling commission into one of the defining masterpieces of the High Renaissance. Its scenes—from the Creation of Adam to the dramatic prophets and sibyls—reset expectations for scale, anatomy, and storytelling in art. The ceiling's impact echoed for centuries, influencing everyone from Baroque painters to modern visual culture.

* * *

NOVEMBER 2

Question: On this day in 1947, what type of committee did the U.S. House of Representatives create that soon became a powerful symbol of Cold War anti-communism?

Answer: HUAC

On November 2nd, 1947, the House Un-American Activities Committee (HUAC) began high-profile hearings that helped define America's early Cold War culture. The committee pursued alleged communist influence, famously targeting Hollywood, labor unions, and government officials. The resulting "Hollywood Ten" contempt convictions and blacklists chilled free expression and careers across the entertainment industry. HUAC's legacy remains a cautionary tale about fear-driven politics and the tension between security and civil liberties.

* * *

NOVEMBER 3

Question: On this day in 1957, which space mission shocked the world by sending the first living creature into orbit and safely returning it?

Answer: Sputnik 2 (Laika)

On November 3rd, 1957, the Soviet Union launched Sputnik 2 carrying Laika, the first living creature to orbit Earth. The mission proved that a living being could survive launch and time in space—an essential step toward human spaceflight—even though Laika did not survive the flight. Internationally, it intensified the Space Race and fueled U.S. pressure to accelerate science education and rocket development. Laika became an enduring, complicated symbol of both scientific daring and ethical debate.

* * *

NOVEMBER 4

Question: On this day in 1922, which British archaeologist first peered into King Tutankhamun's sealed tomb and reportedly saw "wonderful things"?

Answer: Howard Carter

On November 4th, 1922, archaeologist Howard Carter found the first steps leading to Tutankhamun's tomb in Egypt's Valley of the Kings. Backed by Lord Carnarvon, Carter had searched for years, convinced the boy-king's burial remained undiscovered. The find became the most famous archaeological discovery of the 20th century, dazzling the world with intact treasures and vivid glimpses of ancient royal life. It also reshaped modern Egyptology and sparked global "Tutmania" in art, fashion, and popular culture.

* * *

NOVEMBER 5

Question: On this day in 1605, which English Catholic conspirator was caught guarding barrels of gunpowder beneath Parliament in a plot to blow up the king and the House of Lords?

Answer: Guy Fawkes

On November 5th, 1605, Guy Fawkes was discovered in the cellars beneath the House of Lords with gunpowder, exposing the Gunpowder Plot. The conspiracy aimed to assassinate King James I and ignite a political and religious upheaval in Protestant England. After arrests and executions, the failed plot became a national story retold each year in bonfires, fireworks, and the enduring rhyme, "Remember, remember…" Over time, Fawkes's image evolved from traitor to cultural icon, used in protests and popular media worldwide.

* * *

NOVEMBER 6

Question: On this day in 1860, who won the U.S. presidential election that triggered several Southern states to begin seceding from the Union?

Answer: Abraham Lincoln

On November 6, 1860, Abraham Lincoln was elected the 16th president of the United States. His victory, achieved without carrying a single Southern state, convinced many slaveholding leaders that their political power was collapsing. Within weeks, South Carolina voted to secede, and other states followed, forming the Confederate States of America. The election didn't start the conflict by itself, but it lit the fuse that led directly to the Civil War.

* * *

November 7

Question: On this day in 1917, which revolutionary leader's Bolsheviks seized key points in Petrograd, helping topple Russia's Provisional Government?

Answer: Vladimir Lenin

On November 7, 1917, Vladimir Lenin's Bolsheviks launched the uprising that became known as the October Revolution (named for Russia's old calendar). They moved swiftly to seize bridges, rail hubs, and government buildings in Petrograd, then arrested ministers of the Provisional Government. The takeover pulled Russia toward a one-party socialist state and soon sparked a brutal civil war. Its aftermath reshaped the 20th century, setting the stage for the creation of the Soviet Union and decades of global ideological rivalry.

* * *

November 8

Question: On this day in 1895, which physicist announced the discovery of a mysterious new kind of radiation later used to see inside the human body?

Answer: Wilhelm Conrad Röntgen

On November 8, 1895, Wilhelm Conrad Röntgen discovered what he called "X-rays" while experimenting with cathode rays. He realized the invisible radiation could pass through soft tissue but was blocked by denser materials like bone and metal. Within months, doctors were using X-rays to locate fractures and bullets—an astonishing leap for medicine.

Röntgen's discovery launched modern diagnostic imaging and earned him the first Nobel Prize in Physics in 1901.

* * *

NOVEMBER 9

Question: On this day in 1989, the opening of which barrier became the iconic symbol of the Cold War's collapse in Europe?

Answer: The Berlin Wall

On November 9, 1989, East German authorities announced relaxed travel rules, and crowds surged to Berlin's checkpoints demanding passage. Confused border guards, lacking clear orders, eventually opened the gates, and people poured through—celebrating atop the concrete divide that had separated families and ideologies for 28 years. The scenes became an instant global symbol of the end of Communist rule in Eastern Europe. Within a year, Germany reunified, and the Cold War's European front rapidly unraveled.

* * *

NOVEMBER 10

Question: On this day in 1775, which branch of the U.S. armed forces was established to protect ships and enforce laws at sea?

Answer: The U.S. Marine Corps

On November 10, 1775, the Continental Congress authorized the creation of the Continental Marines, the forerunner of today's U.S. Marine Corps. The new force was meant to serve aboard naval vessels, conduct raids, and protect American interests on the water during the Revolutionary War. Early Marines fought in ship-to-ship battles and shore actions that helped give the young rebellion a fighting chance. The Corps later became renowned for rapid deployments and expeditionary warfare —"first to fight" in many American conflicts.

* * *

NOVEMBER 11

Question: On this day in 1918, what agreement took effect at 11 a.m., ending major fighting on the Western Front in World War I?

Answer: The Armistice of Compiègne

On November 11, 1918, the Armistice of Compiègne took effect, silencing much of the gunfire of World War I after four brutal years. It was signed in a railway carriage in the Forest of Compiègne, forcing Germany to accept harsh ceasefire terms. While it ended the fighting, it did not create a lasting peace—those negotiations came later at Versailles. The moment became a powerful symbol of remembrance, commemorated as Armistice Day and, in many countries, Veterans Day or Remembrance Day.

* * *

NOVEMBER 12

Question: On this day in 1936, which engineering marvel connecting San Francisco to Oakland was opened to the public?

Answer: The San Francisco–Oakland Bay Bridge

On November 12, 1936, the San Francisco–Oakland Bay Bridge opened, instantly reshaping commutes and commerce in the Bay Area. At the time, it was among the longest bridges in the world and a showpiece of Depression-era infrastructure. Its original design even carried trains as well as cars, reflecting the era's faith in multi-modal transit. The bridge has since been retrofitted and partially rebuilt for earthquake safety, but it remains one of California's defining landmarks.

* * *

NOVEMBER 13

Question: On this day in 1970, which spacecraft became the first to successfully land on Venus and transmit data back to Earth?

Answer: Venera 7

On November 13, 1970, the Soviet probe Venera 7 made history by landing on Venus and sending signals back to Earth. The achievement was astonishing because Venus is a planet of crushing pressure and searing heat—conditions that destroy most hardware quickly. Venera 7 transmitted for only a short time from the surface, but it proved a landing was possible. Its success kicked off a run of increasingly capable Soviet Venus missions that revealed a hostile world hidden beneath thick clouds.

* * *

NOVEMBER 14

Question: On this day in 1889, which pioneering journalist embarked on a race-inspired journey to circle the globe in 72 days?

Answer: Nellie Bly

On November 14, 1889, Nellie Bly set off from New York to circle the world, aiming to beat the fictional record from Jules Verne's novel. Traveling by steamship, train, and other connections, she turned the trip into a real-time media sensation. She ultimately finished in just over 72 days, becoming a global celebrity and a symbol of daring, modern journalism. The stunt also challenged assumptions about what women could do in public life—especially alone and at speed.

* * *

NOVEMBER 15

Question: On this day in 1988, which Palestinian leader issued a declaration that many cite as the proclamation of the State of Palestine?

Answer: Yasser Arafat

On November 15, 1988, Yasser Arafat, speaking for the Palestine Liberation Organization, issued a declaration of

Palestinian independence. The statement referenced U.N. resolutions and framed statehood as part of an international legal and diplomatic process. Dozens of countries recognized the declaration, though territory, borders, and governance remained contested. It became a key milestone in the long, still-unresolved struggle over sovereignty and peace in the region.

* * *

NOVEMBER 16

Question: On this day in 1532, which Spanish conquistador captured the Inca emperor at Cajamarca, a turning point that helped topple the Inca Empire?

Answer: Francisco Pizarro

On November 16, 1532, Francisco Pizarro ambushed and captured the Inca ruler Atahualpa in Cajamarca. Though vastly outnumbered, the Spaniards used surprise, firearms, steel weapons, and horses to devastating effect. Atahualpa offered an enormous ransom in gold and silver, but he was ultimately executed, shattering Inca political stability. The capture opened the door to Spanish control of Peru and became one of history's starkest examples of how disease, technology, and internal divisions could accelerate conquest.

* * *

NOVEMBER 17

Question: On this day in 1869, what major engineering feat connected the Mediterranean Sea to the Red Sea, transforming global trade routes?

Answer: The Suez Canal

On November 17, 1869, the Suez Canal officially opened, creating a direct sea route between Europe and Asia. The canal slashed travel time by eliminating the long voyage around the Cape of Good Hope. Backed by French interests and built with massive labor, it quickly became one of the world's most strategic chokepoints. Its control would spark international rivalries for generations, influencing conflicts and diplomacy well into the 20th and 21st centuries.

* * *

NOVEMBER **18**

Question: On this day in 1978, which U.S. congressman was assassinated in Guyana while investigating reports about a remote religious settlement?

Answer: Leo Ryan

On November 18, 1978, U.S. Congressman Leo Ryan was murdered at an airstrip near Jonestown, Guyana, after visiting the Peoples Temple settlement. His delegation had gone to investigate allegations of abuse and coercion, and some members of the group tried to leave with him. Hours later came the horrifying mass deaths at Jonestown, where over 900 people died in a murder-suicide under Jim Jones's control. The tragedy reshaped how the public and lawmakers viewed cults, coercive persuasion, and the dangers of unchecked charismatic authority.

* * *

NOVEMBER **19**

Question: On this day in 1863, which U.S. president delivered a brief speech at the dedication of a cemetery after a pivotal Civil War battle?

Answer: Abraham Lincoln

On November 19, 1863, Abraham Lincoln delivered the Gettysburg Address at the dedication of the Soldiers' National Cemetery in Pennsylvania. In just a few minutes, he reframed the Civil War as a test of whether a nation founded on equality could endure. The speech's closing promise of "government of the people, by the people, for the people" became a defining statement of democratic ideals. Initially received with mixed reactions, it later became one of the most quoted and influential speeches in American history.

* * *

NOVEMBER **20**

Question: On this day in 1945, which set of trials began in Germany to prosecute leading Nazi officials for war crimes and crimes against humanity?

Answer: The Nuremberg Trials

On November 20, 1945, the Nuremberg Trials opened, bringing top Nazi leaders before an international military tribunal. The proceedings established that individuals—not just states—could be held accountable for atrocities under international law. Prosecutors documented the Holocaust and other crimes with an unprecedented body of evidence, including film and captured records. The trials helped shape modern human-rights law and set enduring legal precedents for later international courts.

* * *

NOVEMBER 21

Question: On this day in 1620, what agreement did the Pilgrims and other settlers sign aboard a ship to establish self-government in their new colony?

Answer: The Mayflower Compact

On November 21st, 1620, the passengers of the Mayflower signed the Mayflower Compact off Cape Cod. With no clear legal authority to govern them where they'd landed, they pledged to form a "civil body politic" and follow laws made for the common good. It wasn't a constitution in the modern sense, but it set a powerful precedent for government by consent in English North America. Later generations would point to it as an early building block of American democratic ideals.

* * *

NOVEMBER 22

Question: On this day in 1963, which U.S. president was assassinated during a motorcade in Dallas, Texas?

Answer: John F. Kennedy

On November 22nd, 1963, President John F. Kennedy was fatally shot while riding in a motorcade through Dealey Plaza in Dallas. The nation watched in shock as Lyndon B. Johnson was sworn in aboard Air Force One only hours later. The Warren Commission concluded that Lee Harvey Oswald acted alone, but controversies and alternative theories have persisted for decades. The assassination reshaped American politics, accelerated civil rights legislation, and remains a defining moment of 20th-century U.S. history.

* * *

NOVEMBER 23

Question: On this day in 1936, which magazine launched in the United States and quickly became a dominant force in photojournalism?

Answer: Life magazine

On November 23rd, 1936, Life magazine debuted and helped turn photography into mass-market storytelling. Its large-format images brought distant wars, celebrities, science, and everyday life into American living rooms with unprecedented immediacy. Life's photo essays helped define what the public "saw" as the big events of the mid-20th century. Even after its heyday, the magazine's visual style influenced modern journalism, advertising, and documentary photography.

* * *

NOVEMBER 24

Question: On this day in 1859, which British naturalist published a book that introduced natural selection as a mechanism for evolution?

Answer: Charles Darwin

On November 24th, 1859, Charles Darwin published "On the Origin of Species," laying out evolution by natural selection in meticulous detail. Drawing on observations from the Beagle voyage and years of research, Darwin argued that species change over time through heritable variation and differential survival. The book sparked fierce debate, challenging prevailing views about creation and humanity's place in nature. Its core ideas became the foundation of modern biology and still shape genetics, ecology, and medicine today.

* * *

NOVEMBER 25

Question: On this day in 1915, which scientist presented the field equations that completed the general theory of relativity?

Answer: Albert Einstein

On November 25th, 1915, Albert Einstein presented the final form of the field equations of general relativity to the Prussian Academy of Sciences. These equations described gravity not as a force, but as the curvature of spacetime caused by mass and energy. The theory soon explained anomalies like Mercury's orbit and predicted phenomena such as gravitational lensing and time dilation. A century later, it remains essential for understanding the cosmos—and even helps GPS work accurately on Earth.

* * *

NOVEMBER 26

Question: On this day in 1922, which archaeologist first entered King Tutankhamun's sealed tomb in Egypt's Valley of the Kings?

Answer: Howard Carter

On November 26, 1922, Howard Carter stepped into Tutankhamun's tomb after years of painstaking excavation funded by Lord Carnarvon. When asked if he could see anything, Carter famously replied, "Yes—wonderful things," as glittering artifacts emerged from the darkness. The discovery became one of archaeology's biggest media sensations and sparked a global "Tutmania" craze. It also transformed how the public engaged with ancient Egypt, while raising lasting debates about excavation ethics and cultural heritage.

* * *

NOVEMBER 27

Question: On this day in 1942, which major naval battle ended the Guadalcanal campaign and marked a turning point in the Pacific War?

Answer: Battle of Tassafaronga

On November 30, 1942, U.S. and Japanese forces clashed in the Battle of Tassafaronga off Guadalcanal during a high-stakes night action. Although the Americans had radar advantage, Japanese destroyers used superb tactics and Long Lance torpedoes to inflict severe damage, including crippling the USS Northampton. Tactically it was a Japanese success, but it failed to deliver the supplies needed to shift the broader campaign. Strategically, the battle underscored that Japan's position on Guadalcanal was becoming untenable as U.S. strength and logistics surged.

* * *

NOVEMBER 28

Question: On this day in 1947, which colonial territory voted in a UN-supervised plebiscite to become independent Indonesia rather than remain under Dutch rule?

Answer: West Java (Pasundan)

On November 27, 1947, a UN-monitored vote in West Java —amid the chaotic Indonesian National Revolution—was used to legitimize a federal "State of Pasundan" aligned with Dutch plans. The plebiscite became controversial, with many Indonesians viewing it as political engineering meant to weaken the new republic through a patchwork federation. In practice, the effort couldn't stop the momentum toward a unified Indonesian independence. The episode illustrates how referendums and "states" can be tools in decolonization struggles—not just expressions of popular will.

* * *

NOVEMBER 29

Question: On this day in 1520, which European explorer reached the Pacific Ocean after navigating the strait at South America's southern tip?

Answer: Ferdinand Magellan

On November 28, 1520, Ferdinand Magellan's expedition emerged from the treacherous passage now called the Strait of Magellan and entered the vast Pacific. Magellan named it "Mar Pacífico" for its deceptively calm waters—though the crossing that followed was brutal, with starvation and scurvy ravaging the crew. This moment proved a sea route from the Atlantic to the Pacific and reshaped European global navigation. It also accelerated imperial competition across the oceans, linking continents through exploration, trade, and conquest.

* * *

NOVEMBER 30

Question: On this day in 1863, which U.S. president issued a proclamation creating a national day of thanksgiving, helping unify the holiday across the country?

Answer: Abraham Lincoln

On November 26, 1863, Abraham Lincoln proclaimed a national Thanksgiving Day to be observed on the last Thursday of November. In the middle of the Civil War, the proclamation framed gratitude as a civic practice—recognizing hardship while urging national unity and humility. The move built on years of advocacy by writer and editor Sarah Josepha Hale, who campaigned relentlessly for a standardized holiday. Over time, Lincoln's proclamation helped cement Thanksgiving as a shared American tradition with powerful cultural staying power.

1 2

DECEMBER

December 1

Question: On this day in 1955, who refused to give up her bus seat in Montgomery, Alabama—an act that helped ignite the U.S. civil rights movement?

Answer: Rosa Parks

On December 1, 1955, Rosa Parks was arrested after refusing to surrender her seat to a white passenger on a Montgomery city bus. Her quiet act of defiance became the catalyst for the Montgomery Bus Boycott, led by local Black leaders including a young Martin Luther King Jr. The boycott lasted 381 days and dealt a major economic blow to the segregated transit system. In 1956, the Supreme Court ultimately upheld a ruling that bus segregation was unconstitutional, making Parks a lasting symbol of everyday courage.

* * *

DECEMBER 2

Question: On this day in 1823, which U.S. president outlined a foreign-policy warning to Europe that later became known as the Monroe Doctrine?

Answer: James Monroe

On December 2, 1823, President James Monroe delivered a message to Congress declaring that the Americas were no longer open to European colonization. The statement warned European powers that attempts to reassert control in the Western Hemisphere would be viewed as a threat to the United States. Although the young nation lacked the military strength to enforce it alone, the idea gained weight over time —especially with British naval power aligning against new European empires. The Monroe Doctrine became a cornerstone of U.S. foreign policy and echoed through later interventions and diplomacy in the region.

* * *

DECEMBER 3

Question: On this day in 1967, which surgeon performed the world's first successful human-to-human heart transplant?

Answer: Christiaan Barnard

On December 3, 1967, South African surgeon Christiaan Barnard transplanted a donor heart into Louis Washkansky in Cape Town. The operation stunned the world and marked a turning point in modern medicine, showing that replacing a failing human heart could be more than science fiction.

Washkansky lived 18 days, ultimately dying from pneumonia —highlighting how immune suppression and infection would become central challenges in transplant care. The breakthrough accelerated research, refined surgical techniques, and helped build the transplant systems used globally today.

* * *

DECEMBER 4

Question: On this day in 1971, which ship suffered a mysterious disappearance in the Bermuda Triangle and became a pop-culture legend?

Answer: Mary Celeste

On December 4, 1872, the merchant ship Dei Gratia discovered the Mary Celeste drifting in the Atlantic with no one aboard. The vessel was seaworthy, its cargo largely intact, and there were signs of a hurried departure—yet the crew and passengers vanished without a definitive explanation. The case became one of history's most enduring maritime mysteries, fueling theories from piracy to seaquakes to more fanciful tales. Although it's often linked to the "Bermuda Triangle," the Mary Celeste was found far from it, proving how legends can outrun geography.

* * *

DECEMBER 5

Question: On this day in 1933, which U.S. constitutional amendment repealed Prohibition and made alcohol legal again nationwide?

Answer: The 21st Amendment

On December 5, 1933, the 21st Amendment was ratified, ending the national ban on alcohol imposed by the 18th Amendment. Prohibition had aimed to curb social problems, but it also boosted organized crime, encouraged dangerous bootlegging, and overwhelmed law enforcement. Repeal didn't instantly end alcohol-related issues, but it shifted regulation to states and brought production back into the open economy. It remains the only time a constitutional amendment has been repealed by another amendment—history's ultimate legal "undo" button.

* * *

DECEMBER 6

Question: On this day in 1917, what major European capital was captured by German forces after a fierce World War I campaign that reshaped Eastern Europe?

Answer: Jerusalem

On December 6, 1917, British forces under General Edmund Allenby captured Jerusalem from the Ottoman Empire during World War I. The city's fall marked a major symbolic and strategic blow to Ottoman control in the region. Allenby famously entered on foot to show respect for the city's religious significance, a gesture widely reported at the time.

The capture helped set the stage for the postwar remapping of the Middle East under British influence and mandates.

* * *

DECEMBER 7

Question: On this day in 1941, where did a surprise attack thrust the United States into World War II almost overnight?

Answer: Pearl Harbor

On December 7, 1941, Japan launched a surprise aerial attack on the U.S. naval base at Pearl Harbor in Hawaii. The strike devastated battleships and aircraft, killing more than 2,400 Americans and shocking a nation that had been deeply divided about entering the war. The next day, the United States declared war on Japan, and within days Germany and Italy declared war on the U.S. Pearl Harbor became a defining turning point—an instant shift from isolation to full-scale global conflict.

* * *

DECEMBER 8

Question: On this day in 1980, which famous musician was shot outside his New York City apartment building, shocking fans worldwide?

Answer: John Lennon

On December 8, 1980, former Beatle John Lennon was shot and killed outside the Dakota apartment building in New York City. His death triggered an outpouring of grief and public memorials across the globe, with fans gathering in silent vigils and song-filled tributes. Lennon's work—both with The Beatles and as a solo artist—had shaped modern popular music and the cultural politics of the 1960s and 1970s. The tragedy also intensified debates about celebrity, obsession, and gun violence in the United States.

* * *

December 9

Question: On this day in 1965, which country became the first to withdraw from the United Nations, protesting the organization's stance on apartheid?

Answer: Indonesia

On December 9, 1965, Indonesia announced it would withdraw from the United Nations, the first nation ever to do so. President Sukarno's government was protesting Malaysia's election to the UN Security Council amid a tense regional confrontation known as Konfrontasi. The move was more political theater than permanent exit: Indonesia resumed cooperation and formally rejoined the UN the following year. The episode shows how Cold War-era disputes and regional rivalries could spill onto the world's main diplomatic stage.

* * *

DECEMBER 10

Question: On this day in 1901, which prize—created from an inventor's fortune—was awarded for the first time, launching a global tradition of honoring major achievements?

Answer: The Nobel Prize

On December 10, 1901, the first Nobel Prizes were awarded in Stockholm and Oslo, fulfilling Alfred Nobel's will. Nobel, the inventor associated with dynamite, directed his fortune to honor breakthroughs in physics, chemistry, medicine, literature, and peace. The prizes quickly became one of the world's most prestigious signals of scientific and cultural impact. Over time, Nobel recognition has shaped careers, public attention, and even national pride—turning annual awards into a global intellectual event.

*　*　*

DECEMBER 11

Question: On this day in 1941, what country became the first major power to declare war on Japan after the attack on Pearl Harbor?

Answer: Canada

On December 11, 1941, Canada became the first major Allied nation to declare war on Japan, acting independently rather than waiting on Britain's timetable. Prime Minister William Lyon Mackenzie King's government moved quickly as the Pacific War widened overnight. Canadian forces would soon fight in the Aleutians, Hong Kong, and across the broader Pacific and Asian theaters. The decision underscored Canada's growing autonomy in foreign policy during World War II. It also marked the start of a costly, long campaign against Imperial Japan that would reshape Canada's military and international role.

* * *

DECEMBER 12

Question: On this day in 1901, what inventor received the first transatlantic radio signal, famously the Morse code letter "S," at Signal Hill in Newfoundland?

Answer: Guglielmo Marconi

On December 12, 1901, Guglielmo Marconi received a faint but world-changing radio transmission at Signal Hill in Newfoundland. The signal—three quick dots for the Morse code letter "S"—had been sent from Poldhu, Cornwall, proving that wireless messages could cross the Atlantic. Many scientists doubted long-distance radio would work because they assumed radio waves traveled only in straight lines. Marconi's success hinted at atmospheric effects (later tied to the ionosphere) that enable long-range propagation. It helped ignite the age of global wireless communication, from maritime safety to broadcasting.

* * *

DECEMBER 13

Question: On this day in 1577, which English seafarer set sail from Plymouth on a voyage that would become the second circumnavigation of the globe?

Answer: Francis Drake

On December 13, 1577, Francis Drake departed Plymouth, launching an expedition that would circle the globe and cement England's maritime ambitions. The voyage mixed exploration with privateering—raiding Spanish holdings and treasure routes during a period of intense imperial rivalry. Drake navigated the treacherous Strait of Magellan, crossed the Pacific, and ultimately returned in 1580 as a national hero. Queen Elizabeth I later knighted him, signaling royal approval of his daring (and profitable) exploits. His circumnavigation sharpened Anglo-Spanish tensions and foreshadowed the coming clash of empires.

* * *

DECEMBER 14

Question: On this day in 1911, what Norwegian explorer became the first person to reach the South Pole?

Answer: Roald Amundsen

On December 14, 1911, Roald Amundsen reached the South Pole, beating rival expeditions in one of history's most dramatic races. Amundsen's success owed much to meticulous planning—especially his use of sled dogs, skis, and carefully staged supply depots. He planted the Norwegian flag and left a tent and letter to document the achievement. The British expedition led by Robert Falcon Scott arrived weeks later and tragically perished on the return journey. Amundsen's triumph became a landmark moment in polar exploration and a masterclass in preparation under extreme conditions.

* * *

DECEMBER 15

Question: On this day in 1791, which ten amendments to the U.S. Constitution were ratified, guaranteeing core civil liberties?

Answer: The Bill of Rights

On December 15, 1791, the Bill of Rights—the first ten amendments to the U.S. Constitution—was ratified after intense debate over federal power and individual freedoms. These amendments protected fundamental rights such as speech, press, religion, assembly, due process, and protections against unreasonable searches. Their adoption helped persuade skeptical states that the new federal government would not trample personal liberties. Over time, court rulings—especially through the 14th Amendment—extended many of these protections against state governments as well. The Bill of Rights remains a foundational reference point in American law and political culture.

* * *

DECEMBER 16

Question: On this day in 1944, which World War II offensive did Germany launch through the Ardennes in a last-ditch attempt to split Allied forces?

Answer: Battle of the Bulge

On December 16, 1944, Germany launched the Ardennes Offensive—better known as the Battle of the Bulge—catching many Allied units by surprise. The attack created a dramatic "bulge" in the Allied line as U.S. forces fought in brutal winter conditions. Key moments included the siege of Bastogne and General Patton's rapid pivot north to relieve it. When the offensive failed, Germany burned through men and fuel it couldn't replace, accelerating the end of the war in Europe.

* * *

DECEMBER 17

Question: On this day in 1903, where did the Wright brothers achieve the first powered, controlled airplane flight?

Answer: Kitty Hawk, North Carolina

On December 17, 1903, Orville and Wilbur Wright made the first powered, controlled flights at Kill Devil Hills near Kitty Hawk, North Carolina. Orville piloted the first hop, and the brothers completed four flights that day, with the longest lasting under a minute. Their breakthrough wasn't just the engine—it was the control system that made sustained flight manageable. That combination kicked off the aviation age and reshaped travel, warfare, and global commerce.

* * *

DECEMBER 18

Question: On this day in 1865, which constitutional amendment banning slavery was formally proclaimed as law in the United States?

Answer: The 13th Amendment

On December 18, 1865, the United States proclaimed the 13th Amendment as part of the Constitution, abolishing slavery nationwide. It followed years of Civil War upheaval and the Emancipation Proclamation, which had freed enslaved people only in rebelling states. The amendment's wording included a "punishment for crime" exception that later fueled major debates over convict labor and mass incarceration. Even so, it marked a foundational legal turning point in the long fight for civil rights.

* * *

DECEMBER 19

Question: On this day in 1777, which European power became the first to formally recognize American independence by signing a major alliance treaty?

Answer: France

On December 19, 1777, France took a decisive step toward backing the American Revolution after news of the

American victory at Saratoga convinced French leaders the rebels could win. Within weeks, French diplomats finalized treaties that formally recognized the United States and created a military alliance. French money, supplies, naval power, and troops would become crucial to the war's outcome. The alliance helped tip the balance toward victory, culminating in the British surrender at Yorktown in 1781.

* * *

DECEMBER 20

Question: On this day in 1989, which country invaded Panama in an operation that led to the capture of Manuel Noriega?

Answer: The United States

On December 20, 1989, the United States invaded Panama in Operation Just Cause, aiming to depose strongman Manuel Noriega. Noriega, once a U.S. intelligence asset, had become a liability—accused of drug trafficking, election interference, and endangering U.S. personnel. After intense fighting, he sought refuge in the Vatican's diplomatic mission before surrendering in early January 1990. The intervention remains controversial, but it reshaped Panama's politics and signaled a post–Cold War shift in U.S. military interventions.

* * *

DECEMBER 21

Question: On this day in 1898, which scientist announced the discovery of radium after painstakingly isolating it from tons of pitchblende ore?

Answer: Marie Curie

On December 21, 1898, Marie Curie (working with Pierre Curie) announced the discovery of radium, a new element identified through its intense radioactivity. Extracting radium was brutally laborious—requiring the processing of huge quantities of ore to obtain tiny amounts of material. The find helped define the field of radioactivity and opened new pathways in physics and chemistry. It also reshaped medicine through early radiation therapies, even as the dangers of exposure were not yet understood.

* * *

DECEMBER 22

Question: On this day in 1974, which NFL team signed a groundbreaking contract that made him the highest-paid player in pro football at the time, transforming athlete negotiations?

Answer: Joe Namath

On December 22, 1974, Joe Namath signed with the Los Angeles Rams in a deal widely viewed as a landmark in sports contracts. The agreement reflected the growing star power of marquee athletes and the rising business stakes of professional football. Although the Rams would ultimately move on quickly, the moment signaled a new era in player leverage and headline-making salaries. It helped normalize the idea that elite athletes could reshape team finances and the wider sports marketplace.

* * *

DECEMBER 23

Question: On this day in 1913, which U.S. Federal agency was created to serve as the nation's central bank and stabilize the financial system after repeated panics?

Answer: The Federal Reserve

On December 23, 1913, President Woodrow Wilson signed the Federal Reserve Act, creating the Federal Reserve System as America's central bank. The move was driven by repeated financial panics—especially the Panic of 1907—which exposed how fragile and fragmented the banking system had become. The Fed was designed to provide an elastic currency, supervise banks, and act as a lender of last resort during crises. Over time, it became one of the most influential institutions in the U.S. economy, shaping interest rates, inflation, and financial stability.

* * *

DECEMBER 24

Question: On this day in 1814, which treaty was signed to end the War of 1812 between the United States and Great Britain?

Answer: Treaty of Ghent

On December 24, 1814, the Treaty of Ghent was signed in present-day Belgium, formally ending the War of 1812 between the United States and Great Britain. The agreement largely restored prewar borders—meaning neither side won major territorial gains—yet it eased tensions and reopened trade. News traveled slowly, so fighting continued for weeks, including the Battle of New Orleans after the treaty was signed. The war's end boosted American confidence and helped usher in a period of intensified national identity and westward expansion.

* * *

DECEMBER 25

Question: On this day in 800, which ruler was crowned "Emperor of the Romans" by Pope Leo III, reshaping the political map of medieval Europe?

Answer: Charlemagne

On December 25, 800, Charlemagne was crowned "Emperor of the Romans" by Pope Leo III in Rome, reviving the idea of a Western Roman Empire centuries after its fall. The coronation strengthened the alliance between the Frankish crown and the papacy, while also complicating relations with the Byzantine Empire, which still claimed Roman imperial legitimacy. Charlemagne's rule encouraged administrative reforms, learning, and cultural revival often called the Carolingian Renaissance. The title and its legacy helped lay groundwork for what later became the Holy Roman Empire and the medieval political order of Europe.

* * *

DECEMBER 26

Question: On this day in 1941, which British Prime Minister delivered the wartime speech that included the famous line, "Some chicken! Some neck!" after surviving a German bombing raid?

Answer: Winston Churchill

On December 26, 1941, Winston Churchill addressed Britain in a defiant speech after returning from a visit to the United States during World War II. The speech followed a German air raid on his residence at Chequers, and Churchill used the moment to project calm courage rather than fear. His quip "Some chicken! Some neck!" mocked the enemy's attempt to intimidate Britain and became a memorable piece of wartime rhetoric. It helped reinforce public morale at a time when air raids and uncertainty were part of daily life. Churchill's talent for turning danger into resolve made his speeches a key weapon in Britain's psychological defense.

* * *

DECEMBER 27

Question: On this day in 1831, which naturalist set sail aboard the HMS Beagle on the voyage that would later reshape biology with the theory of evolution by natural selection?

Answer: Charles Darwin

On December 27, 1831, Charles Darwin departed England aboard the HMS Beagle, beginning a five-year journey that would transform scientific thinking. While the ship's mission focused on mapping coastlines, Darwin obsessively collected specimens, fossils, and observations—especially in South America and the Galápagos. Those notes planted the seeds for his later insights about variation, adaptation, and common descent. Decades later, he synthesized that evidence into "On the Origin of Species" (1859). The voyage became one of history's greatest examples of curiosity snowballing into a world-changing idea.

* * *

DECEMBER 28

Question: On this day in 1895, which brothers held the first public screening of projected motion pictures in Paris, effectively launching cinema as a commercial entertainment?

Answer: The Lumière brothers

On December 28, 1895, Auguste and Louis Lumière hosted the first paid public film screening at the Salon Indien du Grand Café in Paris. Using their Cinématographe, they projected short scenes of everyday life—simple by modern standards, but astonishing to audiences seeing moving images on a screen. The event is widely treated as the birth of cinema as a public, ticketed experience. It quickly inspired filmmakers, entrepreneurs, and inventors across Europe and beyond. From that small room in Paris, a global art form and industry took off.

* * *

DECEMBER 29

Question: On this day in 1170, which Archbishop of Canterbury was killed inside Canterbury Cathedral after clashing with King Henry II?

Answer: Thomas Becket

On December 29, 1170, Thomas Becket, the Archbishop of Canterbury, was murdered in Canterbury Cathedral by knights linked to King Henry II's circle. Becket had been the king's close ally before becoming a fierce defender of church authority against royal power. The killing shocked Europe—an archbishop slain at the altar was a political and spiritual scandal. Becket was quickly venerated as a martyr, and Canterbury became a major pilgrimage site. The episode also forced Henry II into public penance and reshaped the long struggle between church and state in medieval England.

* * *

DECEMBER 30

Question: On this day in 1922, which new political entity was formally established, uniting the Irish Free State with Northern Ireland only briefly before partition took effect?

Answer: The Union of the Soviet Socialist Republics (USSR)

On December 30, 1922, the Union of the Soviet Socialist Republics (USSR) was officially created, bringing together several Soviet republics under a single federal framework. The new state emerged from the upheaval of the Russian

Revolution and the brutal Civil War that followed. It quickly became a centralized superpower that shaped global politics, economics, and ideology throughout the 20th century. The USSR's rise influenced decolonization movements, the arms race, and the Cold War rivalry with the United States. Its dissolution in 1991 didn't erase its impact—its legacy still echoes in geopolitics today.

* * *

December 31

Question: On this day in 1991, which country formally dissolved itself, ending the Cold War-era superpower and leading to the independence of multiple republics?

Answer: The Soviet Union

On December 31, 1991, the Soviet Union formally ceased to exist, completing a rapid unraveling that had accelerated through 1990–1991. The day before, the Soviet's top legislative body voted to dissolve the union and recognize the newly independent states, with Russia emerging as the primary successor. The collapse ended a decades-long geopolitical rivalry with the United States and reshaped borders from the Baltics to Central Asia. It also triggered massive economic and political upheaval, as post-Soviet countries faced the challenges of nation-building, privatization, and redefining their place in the world.

AFTERWORD

You did it—366 days of history trivia, including the Leap Day bonus. That's a full year of showing up, staying curious, and sharpening your recall.

Along the way, you've revisited turning points, uncovered lesser-known stories, and connected dates to the people and choices behind them. More than a stack of facts, you've built a daily habit of asking better questions about how the world became what it is.

Now keep the streak alive in your own way—follow a thread that intrigued you, visit a museum, or share a favorite "did you know?" with a friend. If this book kept you learning day by day, a quick review would mean a lot—and until the next question, keep turning the page on history.

Want 100+ More Mind-Blowing Stories for Free?

Before you dive into your next book, I have a quick gift for you.

As a thank you for reading, I've put together an exclusive collection of **100+ Interesting Real Stories** that you won't find anywhere else. It is the perfect bite-sized companion to keep the fascination going.

Here is how to get your free copy right now:
1. Open your smartphone camera.
2. Scan the QR code below.
3. Tell me where to send your free book!

Don't have a scanner handy? No problem. You can also download your gift directly at:

bookboundstudios.com/free/facts

Luke Marsh & The Team at Book Bound Studios

www.ingramcontent.com/pod-product-compliance
Lightning Source LLC
Chambersburg PA
CBHW051758050726
47598CB00006B/2332